Anticipating Tomorrow

Anticipating Tomorrow

✦

Living And Making A Living
In The 21st Century

Martin J. Blickstein

iUniverse, Inc.
New York Lincoln Shanghai

Anticipating Tomorrow
Living And Making A Living In The 21st Century

iUniverse, Inc.

For information address:
iUniverse, Inc.
2021 Pine Lake Road, Suite 100
Lincoln, NE 68512
www.iuniverse.com

ISBN: 0-595-31964-5

Printed in the United States of America

Contents

Preface vii

Introduction 1

CHAPTER 1   Medical—The Operating Technology 11

CHAPTER 2   Religion—The Mutable Constant 34

CHAPTER 3   Community—The Slipping Mooring 52

CHAPTER 4   Politics: Changing Perspectives 78

CHAPTER 5   Education—The Democratic Autocracy 94

CHAPTER 6   Jobs—The Affluent Gypsies 112

CHAPTER 7   Retirement—Freedom of Choice 130

CHAPTER 8   Entertainment—The Perpetual Domain 144

CHAPTER 9   Networks—The Insular Association 156

Conclusions 181

About the Author 183

Index 185

Preface

This century is already a bewildering departure from any prior era. Almost everything now works by buttons and most of those "things" are never repaired before they are replaced. Information, once accessible only in great institutions, is now available on your kitchen table. Leisure that previously encouraged social time, now promotes solitary time. Skills, learned early in life and expected to last a lifetime, are quickly obsolete. Towns and cities, often built around those skills, are becoming transient as are their industries. Schools formerly based on predictable populations are becoming trailer camps. Worst of all, everything you buy, right down to a mattress, comes with an instruction book which requires an engineering degree to read. And our values are becoming as transient as our belongings. What in the world is going on?

My father came from a society where horse power was the most recent high technology, to one which was changing as he watched. It was a dynamic never long out of his consciousness. In '30s, he purchased an AM "console" radio-the first in the neighborhood-in the middle of one of the worst depressions in American history. In spite of what was subliminal criticism, my home became a regular Saturday afternoon "hangout" for many of the opera lovers resident in that working class building. By the advent of World War II, only a few years later, we were no longer unique. That radio changed the life expectations of the neighborhood. Still, *change* was expected. What's new now is the *rate* of technological change and what's happening in our lives as a result.

Digital technology has speedily transformed the entire world. What agricultural technology accomplished in ten millenniums, the microprocessor did in one generation. Social prescriptions, retirement, religion, business, military strategy—everything from house design through community, city, and national planning are irreversibly altered. In the context of time span, nothing like it has ever happened in human history.

Most volumes dealing with our future explore "the big picture", i.e., developments from a technical prospective. In this work, there is no intention of detailing complicated new technologies. In contrast, the goal is more one of *reporting* accumulating progressions in the personal picture—how the revolution affects people on the daily level that they live. In spite of the apparent fluidity of our lives, planning is still possible and more necessary than ever before. Preparing to deal successfully with such an upheaval requires insight into its reach and that too is what this book provides.

Introduction

If the wheel was one of the most important inventions in history, money was the runner up. Around the 6th Century BC a man called Croesus was the king of Lydia, a small subdivision of what is now called Turkey. He was rich because a natural amalgam of gold and silver had been discovered there. Money had taken many forms including sea shells, wood, cattle, bronze, and women, to name only a few. But gold and silver were accepted everywhere. Metal was a great barter facilitator because it was actually practical. It could be used and reused. It could also be stored and saved. Lydia also had the advantage of being very centrally located geographically and it was a prosperous center of commerce.

King Croesus apparently was pretty smart as kings go. The metal had to be weighed for every transaction. The king (or his people) came up with a very novel idea. He declared standard weights of gold and silver bars and stamped pictures of animals on the bars, He then guaranteed the content of the stamped bars so weighing and testing was no longer necessary. Croesus also recognized another problem. Ingots of metal were fine for large transactions but most everyday trades were small transactions. He then started to cut the bars into smaller discs (actually ovals originally) and stamped each disc with images. The scheme worked well. The discs started to be used in routine transactions and the stamped discs became more valuable than the unstamped discs, so Croesus was making money literally as well as physically.

The idea spread. Within one hundred years it had reached Greece, and within two more centuries, Rome. Roman coins are still being discovered in Europe, all around the Mediterranean, and even in Great Britain. For the first time in history, people had to assign numeric value to products, to work, and even to time. People had to learn to count if they wanted to prosper. Money helped spark an international trade which by twelve hundred AD was widespread but its use had become very complex. Conversions in Roman numerals from one currency to another, interest charges, fines, and taxes became too cumbersome. Arabic numbers reached Italy where the Italian banking community saw the advantages and switched. The use of Arabic numbers expanded to science, commerce, and even to music. The Arabic number system has remained the dominating system until the twentieth with little or no revision.

In the twentieth century everything changed. Instead of the ten basic symbols of the Arabic number system, microprocessors use "digital" numbers with only two symbols, namely zero and one. Originally intended for computer use (to be more specific—for military use) in conjunction with the digital microprocessor, the combination has permeated almost all other modern activities. They have come to control virtually all industrial process with resulting performance advances in products, communications, entertainment, and even in politics. Knobs have become an anachronism. The simplest devices, from clocks to telephones are controlled by microprocessors. In the very near future people without some level of digital dexterity won't be able to listen to a radio, watch a television program, or cook a meal. Eventually, they won't be able to vote. What is more important to our subject, they might not be able to make a living.

Digital electronics changed more than how we work; they changed what we value. For the first time, knowledge is more valuable than property and the consequences are unimaginable. A college degree is becoming more prestigious than a family pedigree. Microprocessor patents are more valuable than any microprocessor plant. Digital electronics will profoundly change the standards of industry and finance which were accepted as "givens" less than a generation ago. Education and training will become an ongoing process for adults, rather than an interval of childhood. Schools will become as much a community attraction as scenery. Culture itself will become a commercial commodity. The Internet is beginning to intrude cyber space relationships into personal associations. The biggest religious congregations will be on (day to day) Internet, not on Sunday church schedules. The greatest data research facilities are on line, not on shelf.

Television made events anywhere instantaneously available everywhere—on schedule. (More people know the name of the British Prime Ministers than the name of their own congressman and that has enhanced a tourism industry such as the world has never before experienced.) Online news will accomplish the same purpose without the condition of schedule. "Online tours" will make pre-tour testing a form of virtual experience.

With every step there was a loss. The invention of central heating reduced family activity because it permitted life in one's own personal room. Telephones further disengaged families because one could now have a personal life independent of family. Automobiles expanded that horizon beyond the neighborhood. Now the microprocessor has extended our personal boundaries beyond continents. Electronics has stretched its influence to the total human scene. Our neighbors across the globe will become closer, but our neighbors across the street might become more distant. It's all digital.

There were people in the nineteenth century who suggested the patent office should be shut down because "everything worthwhile had been invented". As it turned out, it's only beginning.

Money—the Newest Fossil

The advent of money was probably the most radical innovation in history after the wheel. Money changed education from the luxury of wealth to a critical necessity of life. Over the centuries, it transformed social rank from an inherited advantage to an achievable ascendance. Money also shifted popular preoccupation from the here-after to the here-and-now. It drove art, science, religion, national boundaries, and languages. And money drove lifestyles. The production of money came to be a government's demonstration of power. Whatever the form, all governments have jealously tried to restrict the ability to "manufacture" money because money equated to control.

The effort to control seigniorage (the production of money) has always been compromised by private sources. Ancient banks created money every time they issued a loan—often to their government. The bank's clients created money each time they wrote a "bank draft". Since the Second World War, commercial companies such as automobile manufacturers, equipment manufacturers, travel agencies, retail merchants, all began to sponsor credit cards to help sell their goods and services, and it all added to the non-government creation of money. Like bank checks, using a credit card creates non-government money.

Credit cards already dominate transactions in much of the western world and their use is spreading beyond all borders. Most expenses are now being paid with credit cards of one kind or another. For many, any bill over ten or fifteen dollars is a card transaction. Cards are now available which can access bank accounts without the intervention of any bank personnel and indeed, bank cards are now in common use. Microchips and memory have now gotten so cheap they can be embedded in credit cards, which raises many new possibilities all of which essentially forecast the further dwindling of government issued money. Even petty cash, down to dollars and cents, can be exchanged between cards without any third party intercession, using the on-board memory of the credit card as if it were cash equivalent, which, in fact, is precisely what it is.

Electronic money is not science fiction. Cards are able to be refilled like your wallet. E-money can be "spent" exactly like paper money, leading to electronic banks which have no brick and mortar branches and no tellers. Card sponsors like AT&T, and retail distributors like Sears and JC Penney are issuing automatic loans forcing bankers to reformat the direct loan business. Many other retailers have since followed suit by issuing credit cards in conjunction with a financial institution so they too are in the banking business. Quicken, a software writer, is issuing credit cards, as are many others. "Debit cards" are actually a form of cash which can be loaded from a home personal computer—still without the intercession of bank personnel. (Several states are issuing food stamps on debit cards.)

Debit cards are coming into common use world wide for telephone calls and coin vending machines and for petty cash transactions. Debit cards have many practical advantages with no more security problems than any other form of money. A written check, as an example, requires as much as a dozen "handlings" including a very complex Federal Reserve operation before the check is fully credited and returned to the originator. A debit card requires only two, namely loading the cash and "unloading' the purchase price. Nobody else is involved. The incoming "Smart Cards", i.e., debit cards with an on board microchip, will also be used to record a driver's license, medical data, pharmaceutical information, birth certificate, library cards, insurance information, military information, and much more—perhaps eventually all on a single card.

Banking itself is changing in the face of technology. Automatic Teller Machines (ATMs) are almost universal in Europe, the United States, and quickly spreading everywhere else. But, the new banking venue will be in the home. In today's dominating digital economy, all businesses and soon, all homes will have digital access as a building code requirement like plumbing. Indeed Home Banking software is already being marketed by such firms as Intuit and Microsoft. Customer convenience and service is a very large, perhaps the major factor in the wild spread of electronic money. Moving E-money is easier, cheaper, and usually safer than moving paper money. The "Smart Card" version of money is so imminent Mastercard International bought a 51% share of a British Smart Card company. Many U.S. companies such as Wells Fargo, Chase Manhattan, Dean Witter, as well as many banks have joined the enterprise. Soon card reader terminals will become so ubiquitous day to day charges might become digitalized onsite transactions, as for instance paying the trash bill as you take the trash out. Furthermore, E-money is making it unavoidable for communications companies to be in the money business. They are the basic conduit of the system because electronic money is based on digital communications. For the same reasons, it is making it difficult for banks to remain in the direct banking business because brick and mortar banks are *not* primarily in the electronic communications business.

As an advancement of debit cards, "smart card" technology already exists. There are still problems to be resolved, some of them as simple as who will load the card in the first place and how does one replace a lost card, and even more important, how to maintain privacy with so much personal information available on a single card? Electronic money in particular, raises some political problems as well. For example, how will the government control the *flow* of money if transactions leave no paper trail? How will such transactions be traced for taxes, and criminal activity? On the international scene, how will nations which use U.S. dollars for their own national currencies (and there are many) replace them if the U.S. reduces its' production of paper currency. For the most part these are nations whose populations have never used a telephone much less a credit card.

These are mostly application complications, not technology enigmas. The only real question is probably not *whether* physical currency will eventually be replaced by electronic currency but only the extent and the timing of the event. And it is obvious that when it happens, the effects on every day operations for all of us will be profound. The effects internationally are even more profound. Nations which don't have easy access to the international electronic networks, and who can't, for whatever reason, participate in the electronic money system, will simply be unable to share in the growth of world health service, industry, or even in tourism any more.

And just as an after thought, it is interesting to remember gold based money was a major inhibition to any national growth, development, or even political independence for nations lacking gold. Going off the gold standard was a radical (and dangerous) departure from historic monetary faith but that action freed up economic growth. Electronic money is an equally radical shift from paper. Over a trillion dollars a day traverses the world's internet connections with nothing more than the system's programming integrity as a guarantee. Electronic money can move so fast national economies can be damaged before the national rulers have any opportunity for counter measures. In spite of the unreal aspect to such transactions, people and nations without electronic economy are literally destined to fail.

The Nation—the Financial Geography

"Follow the money" is still sound advice for any investigation of economic events. Until very recently, such research would almost inevitably terminate on Pennsylvania Avenue or Wall Street. Today, inquiries are just as likely to lead to Rio de Janeiro or Tokyo. A bank failed in Indonesia, and billions of dollars were siphoned from the international economy to rescue the institution. A virus jumps from a monkey to a man in Africa and trillions of dollars will ultimately be drained from global growth to control the outbreak. The dichotomy of national monetary policy and national trade policy shrinks in the face of global commerce. A Volkswagen is a German automobile, with parts coming from 16 other nations including the United States. Chrysler is advertised as an American car, but the Chrysler Company is now owned by a German corporation and a significant part of their automobile is actually made in Japan. Chrysler is, in fact, a foreign car and it's no exaggeration to say that advertising any "American" car is a public relations invention. Reebok is a British company, owned by Americans, whose products are produced in Korea.

A very few years ago none of these fiction-like conditions would have been even plausible, much less important, but in a global economy, where the old slogan "Buy American" is meaningless, events everywhere directly affect the price of Wisconsin cheese sandwiches. American business can't be indifferent to the exchange rate of the Euro. American workers can't ignore third world wage levels. The rest of the world can't ignore American GNP growth. Nations were founded on economic advantage and cultural unity but today, those characteristics are no longer enclosed by geography. The dispassionate fact is that the affairs of the entire world immediately affect Main Street, America, as well as Main Street, everywhere else. Corporations will need to think twice about blocking foreign competition because some of the competitors are almost inevitably divisions, joint ventures, or vendors of their own companies. Union members will have to reflect on boycott motions because the ultimate damage they do might be to their own pension portfolios. Cultural isolationists will need to confront a tidal wave of constant borderless exposure. Educational professionals will deal with increasing numbers of American born students who don't speak English. And politicians will be forced to contemplate a porous county line and a receding water's edge.

The most unexpected feature of the information age is the newly opened opportunity for upward mobility which never before existed. It could leave many needed jobs unfilled at entry level with only automation or immigration as possible solutions. For many of them, automation is not cost effective and unlikely. Immigration has been our traditional solution to this dilemma and no country in the world has been more successful at using this strategy than the United States. We are truly a nation of immigrants but in our prior experience, the newcomers were a proportionally small part of our total population and there was enough "open" space to minimize cultural collision. Our culture remained predominantly Anglo-Saxon, Protestant, and European. In this new age, the immigrant's increasing presence will change the demographics of the nation. Mainstream political parties, often infused with racist and nationalist attitudes, are recognizing they are on the losing end of this dynamic phenomenon.

With a more fortunate outlook, the population of the United States, unlike northern Europe, is actually growing but the growth is largely an inflow of non-Caucasian peoples. The increasing presence of non-English speaking, non European newcomers in America will produce both complication and payback. For example, previously homogeneous Main Streets will need to accept fence line neighbors who don't worship as they do, don't socialize as they do, don't eat the same foods they do, don't dress as they do, and don't necessarily have the same moral norms they have. The physical aspect of familiar places will change. The educational needs will change so the instructive process and content will be revised. The politics and the power structure will surely change. Unfamiliar people are always catalysts for new approaches. If there is anything the industrial world will see a great deal of in the next decades, it will assuredly be the unfamiliar.

Those are positives and they are important to Main Street. Aside from many skilled new arrivals, many others will fill low skill, low paying jobs few Americans will accept. The most immediate advantage is contributing financial support to "pay as you go" social programs with increasing numbers of beneficiaries. The Social Security books can't be balanced with slight-of-hand bookkeeping. It requires people—working people. For the moment, at least, the only realistic answer to funding shortages is greater productivity and a larger tax base. Technology will certainly provide the improved productivity, but, under the current construction, only population can supply the tax base. Until someone comes up with a really dramatic alternative, strange people from strange places will be the major source of our population. Main Street and 1600 Pennsylvania Avenue will have to cope with all of it. In a world as interconnected as ours will become, slogans won't ease the transition.

The Economy—the Uncertain Target

For ten thousand years people have been shedding blood over physical resources. Every pretext from God to Destiny was used to justify every imaginable crime committed during those conflicts. Possession and control are what Adam Smith, David Ricardo, Marx, and Engels were all debating in describing their world. Their market construction consisted exclusively of manufacturers and consumers, both of whom were largely bounded by political perimeters. In the global economy, boundaries of any kind are fast disappearing as economic constraints. Suppliers and users are replacing manufacturers and consumers. It is an historic metamorphosis because the most ancient parameter was ownership, and property came to be an absolute standard of law and of culture.

After all those centuries of quarreling, the context of valuation will evolve so dramatically, the very nature of the conflict will change. The paradigm of the equation is intellectual resources, not tangible property. It changes the rules of the game. Manufacturers will no longer want to own the manufacturing process. Their better strategy is having access to it. Product life will be so short that owning process will be analogous to owning obsolescence. "Outsourcing", already a common practice, will outsource the risk of obsolescence as well as financial outlay to vendors while retaining *design* and *marketing* functions, both of which are more flexible and more profitable. Both of them are skill based, and conform to the logic of the future economy which is the exact reverse of even recent corporate strategy. (Rockefeller bought property, rail lines, and coal mines just to control the oil markets.)

The consumers will be faced with much the same predicament dictated by rapid product obsolescence. Low end products can't deal with technology changes such as the switch from VCR to digital DVD which make the "older" device worthless. In those rare cases where repair or conversion might be possible, market support will wane. Higher end products have such short market lives that borrowing the purchase price ultimately results in outstanding loans which exceed the market *value*, not to mention the market *life* of the product. So the new era consumer, like the manufacturer, will out-source the risk by renting the product or the service. Like the manufacturers, they will by-pass the hazard of ownership.

The operative axiom is *access*—access to service, to products, to information, to whatever is deemed currently necessary. Indeed access has become the decisive factor of supply and demand. It's called "Delivery on Demand". The most fundamental consequence of microprocessor modernization is access, not merely automation, nor even efficiency. Information which once required reference libraries or trained professionals is now available, virtually instantly, at home. Online medical information not only provides the known facts, it discloses references, sources, and also allows interaction with expertise, all from the home. Where it once took money, time, and effort, people of similar interest will find each other quickly regardless of geography. Road directions are already instantly available to all. The fundamentalist societies are more concerned about the Internet than they are about any other Western influences and rightly so. The Internet and all the other uncontrollable sources of information are more invasive and far more threatening. And for all of it, access is the fundamental.

If information access will be the key economic component of this age, the real competition—and the real profits—will be for control of them. The competition will not be centered on ownership of cables, and satellites, and servers. Indeed, facility ownership might become a cost of doing business, or even worse, a liability of being in business. Possession of property immobilizes capital. The pattern of outsourcing is not really new. For almost the entire life of the motion picture industry, the race was to own the exhibiting theaters. More recently, the producing studios recognized that the money was in the motion pictures not in the theaters. Today, almost none of the exhibitors are owned by a Hollywood studio. In fact, most of the pictures are being produced by independents and distributed by the studios. Even the great studios like MGM, and Disney are, in fact, "outsourcing" their products, and so it will continue into the future.

On the demand side, the implications are even more evident. A product can be purchased outright with an absolute guarantee of permanent legal ownership. The product may be used for as long as the market supports it, or as long as it is functional. That eventually produces "market saturation". Services, on the other hand, have no substance and are necessarily forever renewable. When your car is serviced, the only absolute guarantee you really have is it will be serviced again. Your telephone bill is for service already rendered. There can be a surfeit of vendors but there is no "market saturation" analogous to that of physical products because there is no necessary limit to service. The ancient adage of science teaches "the more you know, the more you want to know". The market for information demonstrates the tenet.

History in process seldom makes abrupt radical changes. The agricultural revolution took several thousand years to complete. The industrial revolution has taken several hundred years and still is incomplete. The information revolution has, over the course of only two decades, substantially influenced virtually every human being on the planet. A phenomenon with such exceptional historic implications has never before occurred and certainly never disseminated at this velocity. Conversion is going to take a great deal of getting adjusted to and some of the adaptation will be painful because the basic assumptions of many generations will likely be reconsidered.

Any practical judgment of history must include technology via which we all interact every single day and which continues to evolve every day. With the process unfolding more rapidly than at any time in history, it is problematical to make (long term) forecasts, but even now, many near term conditions are already in place. This book will attempt to describe the likely responses to the conversion on Main Street. Our purpose is to anticipate, not judge them. On the other hand, one of the direct consequences of this conversion is more opportunities for many more people. The new era will not be a church bell tolling the demise of the old world. It should more likely be a liberty bell celebrating the overdue arrival of the new one.

1

Medical—The Operating Technology

The medical advances made in the last quarter century are so extensive merely making a short list sounds like science fiction. The purpose of this new research is not to treat disease. [15-see reference material at the ends of chapters] It is disease elimination. Both the new approaches and the pace of developments are accelerating. Medical evolution is, as a consequence, turning into constant transformation, and it should be unsurprising to hear medical costs world wide are rising at several times the growth rate of the world economy. The comparison has not been previously rational because research had been restricted to unendingly finding new ways to treat old diseases—re-engineering old products, so to speak. With the advent of new technologies, the latest thrust is finding new roads, rather than improving old ones. For the first time, medical and industrial productivity can begin to be judged on a comparable basis. Medicine can cure diseases which were fatal in our own lifetime and correct conditions considered untreatable only decades ago. Instruments detect problems long before the patient does. Specialization permits proficiency promotion inconceivable to our parents. Advancement has been so extensive access to that advancement has become a world wide political issue. Indeed, access is increasingly viewed as an "entitlement" even overriding property rights.

[1]Modern pharmacy strategies are perhaps the most remarkable example. Current pharmaceutical therapies are being redirected with pin point targeting. Some block specific cell growth. Some inhibit a tumor's blood supply literally starving the tumor to death. Some even induce specific cancer cells to commit suicide. Most anti-viral agents actually act to prevent infected cells from replicating. Some new medications act to prevent the cell from being infected in the first place. Research is in process to activate the immune system to recognize explicit types of cells as "foreign", such as cancer cells. The aim of the new pharmacies is

so focused they are not effective with non-target cells so the side effects are minimal. "Targeted" pharmacy may be in its infancy, but it is already clear this child is going to be an economic giant. Prescription drug spending is growing faster than any other health allied classification and now accounts for almost 10% of the national health bill. Many designer drugs are already being marketed. Mirapex was an early development, derived from a new understanding of the brain's chemical receptors. Zantec is targeted at histamine receptors in the stomach. High tech as Mirapex and Zantec are, they are not in the class of current efforts. Within the half decade or less, the entire human genome will be detailed, computerized, and almost inevitably recorded on personal "Smart Cards" so pharmacy will be issued specifically designed to match the patient's own genetic system. Such genetically engineered pharmacy will, with equal certainty, begin replacing surgery to the extent surgery will come to be regarded as a pharmaceutical failure.

However, a real news headline in pharmacy is not chemistry. It's quantum mechanics. Smart pharmacies will not merely be unique chemical agents. [7]They will more likely be tiny microprocessors which will control the timing and quantity of drug delivery in response to sensor instructions. If it sounds outlandish, it might be interesting to know that among the many companies working on this delivery system are Motorola and Intel, both notably microprocessor manufacturers. The development is new, but the idea is not. In the 1970's an MIT engineer named Langer developed polymers which could be programmed to dissolve at particular rates. Dr. Langer then teamed up with another MIT scientist named Michael Cima to contain and deliver scheduled doses of pharmacy for long periods of time. It eventually expanded into the ability to deliver doses of *different* drugs on schedule—or as needed. Furthermore, pills already exist with coatings which dissolve in narrowly particular locations such as the stomach, or the intestine, or the colon. Pills are in development which bind to particular tumor cells but ignore other kinds of tissue including other kinds of tumor cells.

And now micro miniature sensors are being added which, as an example, will detect glucose levels in the blood of diabetics. They are the size of rice grains so they can be incorporated in smart pills for automatic drug delivery rates and times. Such capsules are no longer experimental. A great deal of the current effort is being diverted to "finessing" them as for instance, pill production process and economy. When the three functions are combined, i.e., dose sensing, dose delivery, and dose reporting, in an inplantable device or an ingestible pill, doctors will have on site assistance which begins to approach "Fantastic Journey" dimensions. Human testing began as early as 2001. President Nixon's declared war on cancer has met with little real success. For the first time, this dramatically new combination of chemistry and physics is beginning to make the war look winnable.

But, if the pharmacy headline is the introduction of physics, the watchword is Genomics. During the entire prior history of medicine, the goal has been disease prevention or antidote. After such a long record, all the ailments which ever existed still exist, including Small Pox. Every curative victory over those afflictions only shifts the battle site without any expectation of ultimate triumph. Indeed, extending lifespan actually enlarges the spectrum of illness never before seen. Failure to win the war is turning health care into an economic nightmare. Never before has there existed a real hope for disease eradication rather than mere remedy. For the first time in history, there is a unique probability of winning the war not just the skirmishes.

In the early 19th century, a monk named Gregor Mendel hypothesized the elementary mechanics of how genes interact to determine biological outcome. It wasn't until 1953 when two researchers at Cambridge University, Watson and Crick, decoded the actual structure of the mechanism. With the discovery, a research was unleashed which has resulted in the mapping of the entire human genetic blue print which makes humans distinct and each person distinctive. That information has even now permitted the ultimate near term identification of every gene, some 100,000 or more. Instruments and techniques are being developed which will identify specific gene location and function, but equally important, can select single genes from among their hundred thousand neighbors, clone them and amplify them. During the estimated two million or more years of human presence as a discrete species, we have modified everything but our genetic heritage. It is now possible to permanently insert foreign genes or synthetic genes where they did not previously exist. Those techniques are not merely applicable to people, but to all life forms. Indeed, for the first time in history it is not only possible to create and insert engineered genes, it is possible to cross the boundaries of species, a circumstance with some very real ethical problems and equally real benefits.

The current process of "gene splicing" involves using infecting agents, called vectors, rendered harmless by DNA modification, but with a therapeutic gene added to their own DNA. Trials currently in process employ an engineered retrovirus, which only infect cells actually in the process of rapid division—such as brain tumor cells. Other research is directed to determine the reason why some people are more resistant to particular ailments than others. Many of these approaches will fail. The noteworthy fact is that such approaches are now experimentally feasible. Its significance is hard to exaggerate because success might mean the elimination of such chronic conditions as diabetes, muscular dystrophy, and hemophilia.

It's not only the genome of people which are part of this new medicine. Research is underway to determine exactly why one version of an infecting organism is more serious than another. The post World War I influenza epidemic was fatal to millions and then mutated into a version which made everyone miserable, but left most alive. Learning to read the genetic code might make it possible to actually disarm an infecting organism. Genetic literacy, which makes it possible to aim pharmacy at particular cells, will enable a new mode of personal medicine because everyone's genome is almost—but not exactly—identical. Genomics will compel medicine to deal with differences in gender, geography, and ethnicity which, by and large, has been one of the significant failures of past practice. Medicine will finally be able to—perhaps be compelled to—deal with health issues of distinct populations because they will be dealing with distinct individuals.

As if all that were not enough, there are both patents and lab efforts progressing which would substitute replacement tissue and even replacement organs with animal parts, or tissue actually grown from "seed" tissue taken from the patients own body with no immune reaction. There are now half a dozen products in the process of approval for synthetic blood compatible with any blood type and with the added advantages of a much longer shelf life and complete sterility. It's early in this game, and as in all new therapies, there are some risks, but this is another area where money and resources are being expended in huge quantities and where the prospects are growing every day.

[13][15]Indeed, "personal medicine" is becoming so personal the aging variation between individuals is under scrutiny. In 1991 it was found that the tips of chromosomes shorten with each cell replication until there is no tip left to shorten. In 1998 scientists succeeded in artificially lengthening the extremities and managed to extend the life of experimental cells. Even age will fall into the category of "treatable". But extended life has little appeal if the quality of life deteriorates and that aspect as well is undergoing research as never before. For example, brain diseases such as Alzheimers disease were, until recently, the most mysterious maladies of old age. Those illnesses are losing their inscrutability under the onslaught of dedicated research. It is now moderately certain one protein and two enzymes are the activators of the condition. If, and this is still a big if, continued research confirms the theory, then attacking any one of the three molecules would stop development. It doesn't sound like much progress but knowing the target reduces wasted energy, money, and, as in the case of Alzheimers disease, the most valuable commodity—time. Researchers are continuing

to investigate other alternatives as well. Another enigmatic disease with many treatments but no cures was Parkinsons. At least some forms of Parkinson have been traced to a specific gene. Confidence is growing that most such conditions are going to be curable in the near future. Many conditions like Alzheimers and Parkinsons are no longer regarded as an unfathomable and many options are beginning to open up.

Microprocessors are now so common, computers are part of routine medical service. Research groups are designing equipment and programs which will store a person's total health history for instant retrieval. Such equipment will not only make patient data acquisition more easily available, it will put information in the context of the patient's individual history and permit the patient himself to acquire the data in real time with the disease process. Digital equipment is being developed which will transmit life threat alarms to the nearest appropriate facility along with a complete description of the condition, the history, and the location of the patient—all automatically. Typical of such equipment is a pacemaker which *automatically* converts to a defibrillator as required and signals 911, all simultaneously. Smart equipment makes service more economical, and more accurate. X-Ray machines are now not only three dimensional, they are also intensity modulated. It's called IMRT (Intensity Modulated Radiation Therapy) Using this technology, the X-Ray beam is highly focused and changes its intensity as it recognizes tissue density changes so tumors wrapped around normal tissue can both be recognized. Magnetic imaging systems produce detailed views of the smallest incongruities in the most obscure parts of the brain. Lasers are replacing scalpels in surgery and the surgery can be performed without the surgeon even being present.

The technology is proliferating exponentially along with the rising problem of managing the volume of available information to make it useful. Accessibility will be almost as radical as the techniques themselves. The Internet, the data bases, the search engines, the on-line directories, the self help groups, the service organizations, the chat rooms—all allow the latest new therapies to be flashed around the world instantly. Fifty years after the invention of the telephone, most of the world population had never heard of it. Five minutes after the "AIDS" cocktail was announced, requests for information were pouring in from every corner of the world. And the information will not be restricted to professional health care workers. The Internet is not yet quite as user friendly as claimed, nor as reliable but thanks to growing quality control demands, getting better. It helps doctors and their patients instantly research the latest pharmacies, interactions, treatments, and treatment centers. The AMA Council on Long Range Planning reports the percentage of physicians now using the Internet for clinical reasons sky rocketed from something like 20% in 1996 to something like 75% in 1998. Portable devices such as "PalmPilots" make finding patient information faster and more reliable than remembering it while at the same time reducing the number of drug errors.

[1][20]Using the Internet will permit patients to define their personal conditions and it will also encourage them to use their personal means to deal with them. The current estimate is the Internet alone can save as much as $50 billion a year which may not seem like much with an annual health care bill of $1 trillion, but $50 billion can pay for a great deal more research. An informed patient will become a real participant in the therapeutic process. His "demand to know" is, at least in part, being encouraged by the dwindling time doctors can spend with each patient and the increasing share of costs being assumed by patients. [9]Actual patient time with the doctor is now down to something like fifteen minutes with the patient having spent considerably more time in the waiting room. It leaves the patient unable to ask questions, and often dubious about the diagnosis. The Internet is already an alternate source. Alternative sources lead to alternative options such as chiropractic, acupuncture, herbal cures, and even religious cures.

It has to be the ultimate irony that with all this progress, personal health care delivery is becoming a threat to the national health on myriad grounds including ethical, legal, political, AND economic.

The principals of the health market are unique in the long human experience of markets. All other demands can be saturated. All other demands can be separated by wealth factors. All other demands can be segregated by geography. Every other technology reduces costs with maturity. All other markets can be modified by politics and culture. None of those conventions apply to this market. Health delivery is the one absolutely primal demand. All industrial societies have assumed that it is somehow exempted from the market laws on which they literally base their economies. They are all being forced to the realization that technology provides no immunity from old basics and this knowledge has introduced new ones as well.

For instance, if the genes which activate any known disability can be detected in advance of any actual symptom, how will such knowledge affect social reaction? Prospective marriage partners might demand a gene checkout as many do a venereal bill of health? People with cancer genes might feel constrained to do pre-emptory surgery at a time that their physiology is perfectly normal. Abortion attitudes might undergo very dramatic revision.

The immediate concerns will be much more pragmatic. Assembly line medicine threatens to reduce doctors to the status of employee. He must follow the rule book as regards service, diagnosis, treatment, and sometimes pharmacy as well. His income will be determined by "productivity" precisely as is that of any factory manager. Process will become more important than results while paperwork will become even more significant both to get paid and to avoid law suits not to mention possible criminal prosecution. (Current paperwork requires selection from some 10,000 descriptor codes, few of which apply precisely to any one patient.) Even now, doctors needs to order superfluous tests as protection from law suits while being required to limit procedures in order to be paid by insuring agencies. In any other profession, that's called a conflict of interest.

Resistance to this emerging culture is very predictable. Medical school graduates are increasing in total largely due to growing numbers of foreign educated. [21]As much as 40% of the total number of US medical students are émigrés. The traditional source of students—i.e., American born, are choosing other professions or going into research. Furthermore, because of the rise of "procedure de-selection" (i.e., procedures blocked by insuring companies), many of the specialties population, such as cardiology, gastro-enterology, urology, anesthesiology, oncology, etc., will also shrink because the additional investment in specialty training will not be recoverable. The same trend applies to Registered Nursing (RNs). Vanderbilt University research has predicted that the registered nursing population will peak around 2007 and then decline seriously. [21]On the other hand, association between physicians and "Physicians Assistants" (PAs), and other "Non-Physician Providers" (NPPs) will become commonplace. Even pharmacists are trying to be designated as "disease-state managers" for certain types of illness. The NPP is really a new type of health care provider and their numbers, as reported by the Bureau of Labor Statistics, will grow.

The legal factors are no less daunting. When information will be so unconstrained, protecting it will be very difficult. Reverend Joseph Priestly, discovered oxygen but could not patent his work because oxygen is a naturally occurring element. In other words, he identified it but he didn't invent it. On the other hand, several genes associated with abnormalities have already been documented at enormous expense to the researching institution. If the companies obtain patents on these genes, the rewards might be astronomical. The singular new question might then be "who owns the patents?" Like the Reverend Priestly, the company, regardless of the cost, did not invent the gene. Furthermore, the information was obtained from exhaustive research into the genome of many patients. If the victims were the source of the aberrant genes, why don't they too have some legitimate claim on the proceeds of such a patent?

Further on the subject of patents, traditional patents usually had a statistically predictable market lifetime. With new-product market life becoming ever shorter, financial predictions will become unreliable and patents devalued. Legal patent life becomes completely irrelevant when technical generations overlap each other. That might be a growing peril to the continuing performance of this dynamic industry. The final judgment as to patents has yet to been made but research scientists and research companies have already filed for many patents in this very context and so resolution has enormous implications for public health and future practice.

For the patient as well, there are legal concerns. Their problem is personal privacy because it has social, financial, employment, and legal implications, to mention only a few. This very valid anxiety will likely be addressed by more and more laws such as HIPPA (Health Insurance Portability and Accountability Act) which requires health plans and pharmacies to have systems in place to ensure privacy of electronic records. But, if the patient's condition and history is computerized in order to facilitate treatment, who will enter the data and how will it be managed once entered? In a world of instant access, how will legitimate patient rights be protected and what are the legal implications if those rights are breached? As a matter of perspective, privacy issues are not even limited to medical data. The new "Smart Cards" now coming on line will include driver's license, library cards, bank balances, voter's registration, on board cash, as well as health information. With such an abundance of personal data electronically entered—perhaps on a single "smart" card—privacy will become entangled with all the other privacy issues.

And even all of that doesn't cover the investment aspects of the health industry. In a high cost, rapid development market there will need to be short term capital recovery with no secondary market. Costs must be recovered in a single product generation. (The most common example of generational overlap is the new computer which is obsolete at the time of purchase.) Start-up products are always more expensive than succeeding generations, but science in this next era will force almost all new equipment to fall into the realm of perpetual start-ups.

[21]In the year 2003, one out of every seven dollars spent in the United States was spent on health care. The number of beneficiaries is rising because the increasing availability of treatments increases the number of people who can be treated. The number and the cost of procedures are rising because they are increasingly more sophisticated. A tiny percentage of experimental pharmacy

approaches turns out to be beneficial and economically viable, and the few successes must pay for the many failures. [21]When the Medicare system was established in the United States, health care was in a relatively static environment. When the system was installed in the 1960s', seventy years was an average lifespan and health care was 5% of the Gross Domestic Product. Today, there probably isn't a block in any American neighborhood which doesn't have octogenarians. Everyone knows at least one heart bypass patient, and heart and organ transplant patients are numerous. When you lost a limb, it was replaced with prosthesis. We are now at the point where it is beginning to be possible to replace the living limb. If you needed specialty surgery, you had to go where the procedure was available. With robotic surgery, the directing surgeon may not even be on the same continent during the procedure. Elongated life span is exposing medical conditions never before seen. [21]Science has turned out to be far from static with health care at 14% of GDP and growing.

Everyone, from doctors, hospitals, HMOs, and pharmaceutical companies, to politicians has been blamed. The reality is the new advances are the result of huge investment of time, and of talent, and of effort—and of money. And the swelling delivery costs of those advances are far more evidence of success—because there is so much more to deliver—than of greed, certain as it is greed is present.

That environment produced the idea that every condition could be remedied and that everyone was entitled to remedy. [21][22]The illusion of unlimited cure relates "incurable" to "fault". Six and seven figure malpractice awards are common, always with the misconception "someone else" is paying for the award. As a matter of fact, fewer than 5% of practicing physicians are responsible for most of the lawsuits actually launched with fewer than 4% of lawsuits decided in favor of the claimant. This condition is further supported by the practice of "contingency law" where legal fees are due only in the event of success. The patient, has nothing to lose, and everything to gain by filing the suit. A typical malpractice insurance tab was $50 in 1950 and has grown to something like $6000 for a general practitioner and could approach $100,000 for some specialties, all of which a supposed "someone else" pays.

[23]The total American direct health bill for 1960 was about $27 billion, a bill which has increased to just under $1 trillion in the following 40 years. Even after the increase is inflation corrected, the medical GNP of the country substantially outpaces the national economy and is accelerating with time. The Health Care Finance Administration expects a national health care bill of almost $2 trillion by 2007 which could rise to $16 trillion by 2050 (if the annual medical

increase is restricted to 6%—an unlikely outlook). The national reaction up until now, apart from shock, is to control either cost or treatment.

The effort to control commodity cost, otherwise known as "price control", was first attempted by the Romans about 1700 years ago and many times since then. There is not a single attempt from then till now which can be demonstrated to have worked. The first modern line of attack was to control doctor's charges. In 1983, the AMA urged its membership to freeze their charge growth for a year. In spite of the freeze, the over-all health care bill showed no tendency to moderate. The following year, Congress authorized the HCFA (Health Care Financing Administration) to discontinue adjusting their rates against the "cost of living" index with the result doctor's rates increased by only 8% while the CPI (Consumer Price Index) increased by 90% over a thirteen year period. But the increase in the national medical bill continued in double digits because, it turns out, the physicians charges are less than 20% of the total health bill. The doctors are not the culprits of this situation.

The attempt to "control" treatment, now known as "managed care" first appeared in the late 1920's when it was called "prepaid group practice plans". The same groups are now called "Health Maintenance Organization" (HMO). For awhile in the 80's and early 90's they appeared to decelerate the rate of medical cost increase but, as noted, they too began to suffer from red ink and were forced to impose what has come to be labeled "managed denial". This perception has gained enough currency to generate a national debate, now in progress, to enact laws permitting patients to sue their "HMO's" for decisions presumed to be unjustified. Under assault by this legislation are the game rules of this system, where non-professional corporate case auditors determine which treatments are "recommended", a euphemism for "permitted". For corporations, it is absence of profits. As a matter of record, in 1988 about 70% of HMO's themselves were equity funded entities whose stock holders were the general public—the very same people who demanded unlimited service. They also expected the same performance from their HMO stock as they did for any of their other investments. In 1999, half of the HMOs reported losses in aggregate totaling almost $200 million for the industry and many of them, particularly the smaller ones, are withdrawing from participation in this market. So the HMOs are also not the evildoers here.

The emerging outcome of this cost control effort seems to be becoming a market driven health industry which may be only peripherally associated with patient condition. The first question asked of a patient is routinely "how will you pay?" not "how do you feel?" Personal health is measured by absence of illness. For corporations, it is absence of profits. Jobs are rapidly becoming the second casualty. The exploding cost of health programs are forcing more and more corporations to choose between employee health insurance and profits. It has been estimated that the rising cost of employee health care insurance has cost almost two hundred thousand jobs in the auto industry alone—and that was before the current recession.

As an additional complication in a situation abounding in them, there are some 45 million Americans who have no health care insurance at all. In fact, the US has the largest percentage of uninsured population among the industrial nations and over 60% of the uninsured are employed full time. The uninsured usually end up in emergency rooms long after onset, with the rest of us paying the augmented bills.

Just to put the situation in some context, this is hardly an "American problem". The German health care system, which actually started in the 1800s with Bismarck, forces doctors to see something like 100 patients a day and is still in danger of bankruptcy. The British system has treatment delays so extreme that private health insurance is the fastest growing industry in England. Fifty eight percent of British surgical patients wait more than a month for treatment compared to less than twelve percent of U.S. patients. Canada is almost the "icon" of health delivery systems but the Economist Magazine reports Canadian doctors and pharmacists have actually gone out on strike. Many patients opt to come to the United States for treatment for which they personally pay rather than waiting, often fruitlessly, for free treatment at home. In many cases, the national treatment which they finally do receive is either obsolete or inadequate, usually from health professionals they don't know and have not chosen. Few of the European health professionals are optimistic about their system's future performance. With all its inadequacies, the United States remains the absolute leader in health delivery, research, pharmacy development, and results.

The effects of cost containment are already very evident. Many operations are treated as out-patient procedures. Women are sent home only hours after delivering babies. Early discharge is now a general rule. Many hospitals no longer charge for daily care but have adopted a procedure called "unbundling" wherein they charge separately for every aspirin, and bar of soap. The next step, announces the grim humor, is pay bed pans. For the uninsured, diminished emergency room facilities is a particularly dangerous outcome. In spite of all of these counter-measures many hospitals are closing due to an occupancy rate which has fallen to an average of 62%, and are reducing the number of beds. This is particularly affecting underserved areas. For those remaining open, the effects are almost as harmful including reduced staffing, less supervision, and lower skill levels. What makes all this even more confusing is the cross directions of the industries' trends. For instance, the improving pharmacies will cut the length and the need for hospital stays, but at the same time those patients who will be hospitalized will be more ill and will need more specialized care. The hospitals will need to provide a broader spectrum of services but there will be fewer professionals around to provide them.

As an additional complication to this already complex situation, global health will become a distinct national concern. Vast movements of people and cargo will force all industrial societies to recognize off-shore diseases as an on-shore threat to public safety even aside from any humanitarian considerations (as witness the "SARS" outbreak). As a consequence, third world politics and policies will become very much an industrial world problem. For instance, illiteracy is a very clearly health related problem, which, for most of the third world, is possibly the largest single source of the AIDS epidemic. Financing health care is an even worse problem in the third world than it is in the industrial world. Developing countries have 84% of the world's population but spend about 11% of the worlds' health care bill. Therefore, for obvious self interest, the U.S. and the E.U. will become increasingly involved in both foreign education and health policies as a bare minimum.

For better or for worse, the U.S. government is now the major health care vendor. It is also manifest health care cost inflation will drive services to be rationed because there is, at this point, no other option. Since those two certainties are mutually exclusive, it is equally inevitable the mechanics of health care delivery will be significantly altered and that, at last, brings us to the subject of this book. Millennial approaches abound including policy, systemic, and behavioral. Everyone has one, usually cut to fit his own shoulders. Policy solutions are always the publicized routes because policy is the one course politicians assume they can deal with.

1. A very practical, and on its face, a very obvious imperative, will be an increase of financial and educational incentives for mass based preventatives such as inoculations and behavioral risks which can be minimized or avoided. (And even this one is not simple. Inoculations have safety considerations. Automobile safety is related to fuel economy.)

2. The populist solution is to simply pump more money into the system from general revenues. Long experience both here and abroad, abundantly illustrates only one outcome, a rise both demand and costs. No one values what is free or cheap.

3. Price control is still another populist proposal. Medicare is actually an indirect form of price control. It clearly is not working as a budgeting constraint because the problem is not the cost of conventional treatments. It is the mounting charges of new procedures.

4. A supply side proposal is providing more suppliers—doctors, technicians, equipment, etc., has also failed in practice. Back in 1971 the federal government decided the inflation of health care costs was, at least in part, due to a shortage of doctors. Congress therefore passed the Comprehensive Health Manpower Training Act of 1971 which, among other things, provided payments to (medical) schools for increases in enrollment. In 1976 the Health Manpower Act reversed course and actually restricted the inflow of foreign graduates into the United States. It was simply overwhelmingly evident the energy driving sharply mounting costs was amassing medical technology, not scarce personnel. (Though there turned out to be other benefits to this plan—particularly physician availability—competition was not demonstrated to work, given the present system construction.)

[2]Consumers with little or no responsibility for payments simply increased the use of services as they were made more available. This has been statistically demonstrated in a study done by Dartmouth University and published in the Journal Health Affairs of Feb, 2002 which compared different and similar income groups, ethnic groups, age groups, and even geographic groups. The observed result was the eruption of higher paid specialist conferences with even higher costs to the system. But while this strategy (more doctors) didn't previously do anything for national health care cost containment, the ancillary future benefits included improved nursing home care, and more willingness to practice in underserved neighborhoods, greater willingness to adjust working hours to the patient's convenience, and, most important, increased incentives to join health service groups rather than mere partnerships.)

5. Increasing accessibility also includes more "smart equipment" and no action would make a bigger dent in the supply and demand problem. By its' very existence it will produce a revolution in delivery systems as machine trained technicians increasingly operate the machines. "Smart" equipment relieves the attending physicians of routine work and reduces the need for specialists which now constitute more than 60% of all physicians and trending up.

Smart equipment, already appearing, will even open opportunities for patient self care. Such gear will permit automatic monitoring and dosing as needed. Automatic monitoring will provide warnings to the patient and alert standby personnel in emergency centers and ambulances. Smart machines and remote controlled gear will be mounted on mobile units which can operate in underserved neighborhoods. Their operators demonstrate greater willingness to accommodate working hours and have more incentives to join neighborhood "health fairs".)

6. Another suggestion has been to "slow" the endorsement rate of new treatments and therefore slow the rate of accruing costs. Here too, some such system is already in place. The money and time cost of getting test data with professional endorsement is very high. In fact, the elapse time is now generating political pressure for "reform" of the system in order to translate experimental treatments into practice sooner. HMOs are notoriously slow to approve "experimental treatments" but foot dragging is becoming increasingly politically impractical and will be no more effective than price control.

7. A more probable alternative will be a rationing plan. We do, in fact, already have some such rationing but the people devising the rules are the wrong people because, as often as not, they are trained only in bureaucratic procedures. Medicare and HMO's decide which procedures they will accept and which they won't pay for. Personal choice is a long, and a more socially acceptable tradition in America. Devising an alternate system which produces a list of alternatives would significantly modify the lifetime cost profile of individual health choices. It needs to be an individual rationing system which substantially improves everyone's health protection and personal choices, independent of their economic circumstance, and a system moreover, which is sustainable. The system won't be based on everyone getting *equal* care but rather, on everyone getting *maximum* care.

It will need to address the basic problem of the millennium health delivery system, namely unlimited demand and limited supply. Posturing about "lock boxes", and congressional hearings, and law suits are only the appearance of action or as Shakespeare said centuries ago, "much sound and fury, signifying nothing". And so the second rung in this ladder is changes in the health care system.

System ideas are also on the floor from a number of qualified sources. The most traditional suggestion, based on frustration or the desire to "go back to where we started", is quite simply to phase out the entire system of publicly funded or supported health care. We won't spend any time arguing this one because any politician who even jokes about it couldn't get elected county dog catcher the next day. This public reaction is so uniform it is politically dangerous to even investigate most of the actually feasible alternatives which might begin to identify acceptable *and sustainable* solutions. Never-the-less, at least parts of most of the suggestions are likely to reach daily life in the next few decades.

The most probable suggestions, in clear rejection of third party management, are premised on driving health service economics closer to household economics. The immediate purpose is to remove those determinations from the hands of corporate or government discretion.

One approach provides cash allowances to the patient rather than providers but leaves the decision of how to spend it to him. The assumption is that as long as health services are perceived to be "free", unlimited use will grow. In so doing there might be several expected harvests, well documented by long experience, that individual economic decisions are usually more directed than government policies. Reducing mandated government influence also diminishes government operations and at least some of the indirect costs of medical decision making.

Another idea is to give employees the total monies their employer now spends on their health insurance and also give them the same tax credit the employer got for providing the insurance to the extent they actually spend the money for health and health insurance purposes. This takes the employer out of the health business, cuts his cost of doing business, and gives the employee total control of how the money is spent and which program best suits his needs. Such an arrangement reconstructs the association between the patient and his service. It also provides direct inducement for employees to be more economical in their use of health service systems. Even more important, this introduction of personal economics into health care will provide powerful incentives to practice healthier lifestyles and preventative procedures because the famous "they" won't be paying for poor choices.

A. [21] One of the serious variations in this latter category is what is called "capitation" (or sometimes referred to as "defined contributions" programs). In this construction providers are actually pre-paid a set annual fee for each client which covers any and all health costs. In effect, this becomes a single payment program instead of a single payer. It sounds very much like another "insurance" type program except it is the providers who are being paid the fee, not a third party. Capitation encourages the formation of provider networks that encompass most, and possibly all of the skills and equipment required for a modern health maintenance program. A provider network's self interest is to keep the client healthy in contrast to an insurance company which profits by limiting treatment. (Provider network income per client is fixed regardless of the number of visits.) On the other hand, the provider has an income even in the event his patients are perfectly healthy and only show up for annual examinations. The system would need to be built so as to prevent "cherry picking" healthy clients but clients usually come in families not all of whom have the same level of health. But here too, the system would need to be structured with some rationing system in order to minimize trivial use.

Contracting with Provider Networks might introduce several functions now absent from the current scene of insurance contracts. The most conspicuous patient benefit is the elimination of third party interference in the chain of command. Another, perhaps less obvious, advantage would be the patient's access to second opinion without the necessity of leaving the network. The network itself would facilitate consulting, and act as a kind of quality control. An additional patient advantage includes cost predictability combined with personal choice. Giving the patient alternatives promotes provider competition, a here-to-fore unattainable free market disposition in the health industry.

From the doctor's point of view, Provider Networks would offer financial momentum and reduced administrative costs. Relative freedom from individual lawsuits would surely be a fringe outcome of no mean consequence. And still another physician outcome from such arrangements would be regaining greater control of both his cases and his case load. For all of these very same reasons it might be in the self interest of local hospitals to join forces with several such groups. Furthermore, this kind of "insurance" group in combination with the new technologies will enhance "in transit" medical procedures. Those technologies within such a group would permit "on site" health maintenance procedures thus reducing the use of far more expensive emergency room facilities now employed for such purpose.

There would be advantages to the nation in the context of more realistic cost containment stemming from the growth of such practices. On site mobile facilities might also provide lifestyle training, particularly in poor neighborhoods where stationary facilities don't exist. Furthermore, Capitation motivates providers to introduce healthy life style training and furnishes the spread of expertise which can supply it. And certainly, this type of organization would minimize the current trend toward ordering unnecessary procedures.

And, hardly least, Capitation eliminates of the middle bureaucracy.

B. [2]Another recommendation, very controversial but almost universal, is to gradually have people pay an increasing share of health care costs so as to compel them to economize with service in the precise same way they must economize in every other aspect of their lives. The capitation approach, with its high level of predictability softens the impact of greater personal financial contribution. Such a proposal would have a number of fringe requirements.

1. Practitioner rate schedules and credentials would need to be published as they are in every other type of service, in order to permit the potential patient to "pursue" the best deal as he does for any other need.

2. Practitioners would need to do as much as possible for each patient rather than "unbundling" necessary service into separate specialties.

3. Introduce Tax Deferred Savings Accounts and stepped vouchers in order to level the medical playing field for various levels of income. These accounts would be exclusively redeemable by certified provider groups.

4. Introduce a tax adjusted high deduction mandatory major medical policy for catastrophic illness would be a kind of seat belt requirement.

5. Sponsor education programs emphasizing "wellness programs" which tend to prevent or mediate illness and encourage healthy living such as exercise, abstinence or "safe sex", sports promotions, nutrition training, etc.

6 Sponsor corporate tax incentives for wellness programs providing real motivation for employee participation. (This has been a Japanese practice since the World War II)

7. Local tax incentives for constructing bicycle paths and encouraging campus type community developments where people can walk or cycle to school, to work, and to recreation. This would improve health standards through exercise and positive environmental results. Bicycling to work is almost common in Europe where gas is expensive.

8. Phase out passive or active support for polluting, unhealthy, or dangerous products which become public health care issues.

There are groups for which none of the shared cost initiatives will work. Many of these people are undocumented aliens and individuals who, for whatever reason, do not even have access to Medicaid. Some simply live in rural areas where modern technology is not available. Regardless of whether we have any legal obligations to them, the fact is they use medical facilities. Their access to the system is the emergency rooms, always the most expensive route and usually late in a condition which would have been much more economically dealt with early on. For this group in particular, healthy lifestyle education is essential. It is also obvious the emergency room is clearly not the way to deal with the problem. Aside from enforcing the immigration laws more effectively, workable long term proposals, and/or short term palliatives have yet to surface.

Summary:

We are discussing new technology introductions in terms of their consequence on this century's daily life. Health care and its' delivery is an issue at the heart of how this country is going to live. Due to the pace of technology, we will need to make very abrupt adaptations to a wholly novel condition. As usual there's good news and there's bad news. The good news is life span will be longer—probably considerably longer—life quality will be much better, and access will be far wider.

The bad news is we are going to change the way we do medical business which will mean some painful accommodations. Health care is as proper a national concern as the value of the dollar. In fact the two are inextricably linked. Notions of eliminating the federal engagement in ensuring availability are as unrealistic as notions of repealing the Federal Reserve Act and indeed the vocal proponents of both are often one and the same people. But having said it, fiscal irresponsibility will be as medically dangerous as neglect. It is clear the inevitable role of government in this era will be logical access combined with cost control. This realistically translates to increased personal and public financial participation. Simplistic placebos like "market solutions" and "single payer" programs promote ideologies more than they serve health care but the ultimate resolution will undoubtedly include both market and national components.

Rising health care costs will be the second millennial issue. Regardless of source, costs will impact all of us individually. There won't be any "them" out there. The "them" will be us. This is going to be a time when health care budgeting is going to become a routine part of household budget management.

The end of the "health equality" attitude in the future will also end the notion of good health as an entitlement. While patient's rights legislation will widen access to procedures, it will narrow the window of malpractice. This will add impetus to the need to "cherry pick" carefully from among health service organizations without the interference of non-professional personnel. Excepting the singular cases of the elderly, and patients incapable of making optimal choices, this will be still another factor in the personalized medicine of the future.

The public will demand and receive expanded disclosure of health service organizations, their area of competence, as well as their outcome performance, personnel qualifications, and facility identification. For obvious reasons, health care will never be a completely "market driven" industry, but this is a field where competition **is** going to play a greater role.

Server directories will become as common as telephone directories with much the same functions—namely locating sources for particular categories of specialties. These information directories will very likely eventually also assume a form of "Consumers Union" role in rating the organizations they list. Medical service directories have been around since the 1980's as an information source but the new era is evolving them into a type of outcome rating listing available to the general public.

Probably the easiest and the most certain of the market components will be a huge expansion of "smart" machines which will permit market growth of self-help type of equipment such as blood pressure monitors, blood chemistry monitors, infectious agent monitors, etc., with automatic alarms and emergency calls capability. Use of these new devices will require varying levels of patient education and discipline to be effective but they will be far more potent in early crisis detection than any conventional current practice.

Genetic research will also shift much practice toward eradication rather than cure. While the growing reach of individual genetically based prediction, diagnosis, and remedy will enhance cure/cost ratios, an obverse side of this new science is that the patient's role, his decisions, and his share of costs will rise substantially at the same time his connection to particular doctors might be diminishing because of his freedom to "shop" for "best buys". Consumer considerations will include realistic expectations with the most all inclusive listings for "one stop" shopping and outcome comparisons. Disease elimination research will require great soul searching as regards arcane attitudes such as abortion and stem cell research as well as traditionally unlimited privileges such as weapons and disabled person driving permits. Unhealthy life styles are going to become a public concern.

Health care will actually become more personalized. Health maintenance operation will probably be organized around single pre-paid provider associations with clear responsibilities. Collaborative teams of inclusive skills and resources will supersede commercial insurance corporations whose only skill is record keeping. Organizations such as the "National Patient Safety Foundation (NPSF) are assembled by diverse combinations of medical professionals, public safety experts, and public leaders, specifically to establish rules of the road as regards such considerations as preventable error, and error reporting, as well as public and physician education for this evolving market. Patients will have the opportunity to pick and choose their own health agency and to switch if they are not satisfied. The associations will, as a result, become much more competitive. The pre-paid broadly based organizations will be the operational mechanism of this era as part of the effort to make the national medical bill predictable. These health organizations will be doctor-led groups which have a vested interest in maintaining client health because the prepayments are the only income they will receive each year.

Technology will permit much more in-depth patient education and self monitoring, more effective self-care and more trained technicians care. Patients will become an intrinsic part of the "wellness sequence" and will need to learn some basic modern skills such as Internet access to be able to optimally use smart equipment. Education will become a wellness facility. The educated patient will be more likely to have better outcomes because he will become part of his own "health team" by being motivated to ask questions and follow regimes while being less likely to be disappointed with the results. (Experience has demonstrated informed, participating patients are much less likely to sue even when mistakes are acknowledged.)

Technology will reduce the need for surgery by substituting less invasive techniques, while permitting earlier recognition and intervention. At the same time the technologies will permit more effective surgery. Medical talent and equipment will become more available on mobile as well as long distance platforms so procedures now only available in urban centers, will reach rural and poor communities.

Additional bad news is patients will pay an increasing proportion of medical costs.

The bad news is that the pressure towards "productivity" will force doctors to see more patients per day and will deteriorate the traditional doctor—patient relationship.

The bad news is that technology ultimately erodes personal options. Personal behavior is a major contributor to the dilemma. The American Medical Association reports the leading annual causes of morbidity and mortality are tobacco (approximately 400,000), diet/inactivity (approximately 300,000), alcohol (approximately 100,000), infectious diseases (approximately 90,000), toxins (approximately 60,000) firearms (approximately 35,000), sexual behavior (approximately 30,000), vehicles (approximately 25,000), and drug abuse (approximately 20,000). They estimate over 70,000 people die each year from immune-preventable diseases. All of these numbers can be substantially reduced by behavior modification. Insulation from costs permits people to behave irresponsibly without penalty but with great impact on the national medical bill. Bad behavior, unhealthy life styles, and poor environment management make local problems have national consequences. Smoking, drinking, drug addiction, and violent behavior are neither personal nor local if governments are footing the bills.

Among the battered personal options will be the realization that equal health is not a practical expectation. Lawsuits are not a medical remedy, but they are clearly a medical expense. The fear of lawsuits based on disappointing results, or even reasonable human error, is one of the influencing factors for the cost of medical programs. Conversely, the medical field will be obliged to accept expanding quality control standards, and quality standards will impose legal margins on liability. Quality standards and tort reforms will be necessary footings to medical progress and to broadening access to progress.

It is crystal-clear along with all the radical new technologies, medical delivery is going to undergo equally radical changes. Medicine today is on the threshold of a crucial new aspiration. The health care model of the oncoming period will be disease elimination, **not** prevention, or even cure. The altered purpose dictates new relationships between patients and providers. But there will also be many new problems of ethics, morality, and legalisms deriving from the new direction. Eugenics, genetic engineering and patenting, cloning, all raise problems which never existed before, along with new opportunities.

There is, as always, a cost to everything and in one way or another, the cost will be paid by the entire community. The real price of medical services is increasing at a rate even the nation as a whole cannot long sustain. Until something better shows up, technology is the most practical way to restrain the medical outlay produced by the same technology. Unquestionably, the technology will be available, but there are cultural and behavioral accommodations which will need to be made. Those changes are going to have as much influence on the millennial street as the economics which has dominated this chapter.

We really had two problems in the past, one of technology and another of finances. There has been so much progress in medical science that discovery is now more a matter of time than technology. If the technical momentum was attained in the last century, the financial momentum will certainly be reached in the twenty-first. And that is the great news for the millennium.

Reading and Reference:

[1]—*21st Century Miracle Medicine*. Wyke

[2]—the *Grand Disguise*..W.C.Waters III, MD

[3]—the *Health Care Solution*..Dauner & Bowker

[4]—*Health Care and the Changing Economic Enviro*nment. A.L.Sorkin

[5] *Renewing the Promise*. Blumenthal, Schlesinger, & Drumheller

[6] AMA: www.ama-assn.org (312) 464-4442 News & Info Service/Ross Frazer (312) 464-5000

[7] *The Programmable Pill*. Alexandra Stikeman [*Technology Review Magazine* 5/01/01]

[8] *Health Care Costs*. W.B.Latham. M.D.

[9] *Interactive Week*, 3/19/01 "Vital Signs", Bill Scanlon

[10] Atlanta Journal Const.4/25/99 Health Care, Rebecca Rakoczy, P G1

[11] *Time* 1/11/1999 12—American Medical Association, Long Range Planning & Development

[12] NYTimes book revies of "the invisible Heart by Nancy Folbre Sunday, 7/1/ 2001

[13] *The Elderly, Opposing Viewpoints* Bender & Leone 0 89908 450 8

[14] *Extending Healthcare's Reach* Samuel K. Moore, Assoc. Ed. *IEEE Spectrum Magazine* Jan.2002

[15] *Cheating Death*, the Promise and the Future Impact of Living Forever Cetron & Davies 0 312 18065 9

[16] *Newsweek* January 1, 2000

[17] *Newsweek* June 24, 2002

[18] *Time Magazine* January 15, 2001

[19] *Time Magazine* November 8, 1999

[20] *Civilizing the Internet* J.M.Kizza 0 7864 0539 2

[21] *National Practitioner Data Bank (NPDB)*

[22] Medical Malpractice Referral Network

[23] Office of Actuary at the Centers for Medicare/Medicaid Services

2

Religion—The Mutable Constant

The American Protestant group was long fragmented but in the latter part of the nineteenth century three fundamentalists named Finney, Moody, and Billy Sunday initiated an even more splintering revision of American religious practices. After the Civil War, a new expression of religion with a novel form of ministry appeared. At its inception, this variation espoused support for local church activity but very soon became an independent and very unconventional institution. It came to be called Revivalism. It originally had no permanent structures or indeed, structures of any description. Revival meetings were held in tents, in barns, in temporary edifices, or even in open fields. People who attended revival meetings didn't actually know the preachers personally except by reputation. The preachers themselves were frequently itinerant—i.e., they migrated from location to location. Their mission was not to teach Christianity so much as to save souls.

Finney, Moody, and Billy Sunday not only changed the content of what was taught, they changed the context in which it was taught. Post Civil War America began to run out of "free land"—i.e., land distributed by the government. Without mortgages, marginal farms could sustain families, but when the free land ran out, it had to be purchased which meant rising land prices and mortgages. In the 1880's the price of farm land finally began to drop and the farmers suddenly were paying very high loan rates—sometimes as high as 20%—for land worth far less than the face value of the loan. Many farms were no longer viable and the loans were foreclosed. At the same time America was industrializing. Factory wages were rising while farm income was falling. The predictable consequence was that Americans began to urbanize. [2]Immigration and the move to cities and towns separated people from their family roots and revivalism helped solve at least part of their problem. Revival attendance was not a congregation at all. It was actually more like an audience. The revival encounters were, by necessity, non-denominational and they soon became anti-denominational. They began to compete for funds with established churches. A revival preacher's success derived from his personal charisma and their following were increasingly personal rather than doctrinal.

[7][14]The leaders were not necessarily trained in religion, and sometimes not trained in anything at all. Not being ordained ministers, the revivalists called themselves "preachers". The preacher's lack of formal religious education was actually a subliminal attraction for many who had little education themselves. [2]The mission's nomadic character was another attraction for new arrivals in their communities. Those circumstances combined to reduce the traditional shared content of the religious message in favor of concentration on "salvation". In short, faith, not works, was emphasized. The preacher became a partner in faith rather than a teacher of creed. The size of the preacher's audience became visible evidence of his success at saving souls. And, of course, larger audiences meant larger collections.

[14]It was Finney who first recognized changing times and changing needs. He was a very fervent and sincere Christian who exhorted preachers to use any legal means to successfully spread the message. He emphasized results were more important than details insisting "he that winneth souls is wise". He emphasized salvation by conversion, not deeds or creeds. He democratized redemption but did so at the cost of intellectual content, a major departure from traditional religious practice. He also introduced business techniques to preaching. Others soon picked it up. Dwight Moody was a strong supporter of Finney and followed his lead in being anti-denominational. He had more interest in entertaining performance than in elite ritual. He expanded advanced business planning in the revival spectacles including program planning, advertising, scenery, and event story lines as well as trained professional support staff for all of those functions.

Billy Sunday was another revivalist, perhaps the most famous of the early twentieth century (he died in 1935) who was so concerned with his business efficiency his organization was actually once ranked among the top five business organizations along with Standard Oil, U.S. Steel, and National Cash Register. Reverend Sunday turned revival meetings into a kind of American theater which included choirs, professional conductors, soloists, and public relations directors. He gyrated wildly during his performances and often expressed hostility toward ordained ministers (a title he detested) of more composed demeanor. Those attitudes re-enforced a general anti-intellectual aura increasingly associated with the evangelical community to this day. Sunday had the absolute conviction the individual was a morally free agent who could "save himself" and that God rewarded salvation right here on earth. Success was avowed to be the visible evidence of redemption which, in a very direct way, made Sunday a kind of business partner to his more successful followers for which service he expected a return in the form of donations.

Preaching became entrepreneurial using all the business tools such as show and tell, politics, advertising, organization, favoritism, and charm. As a matter of experience, anyone with the right personality, energy, and the charisma could, and many actually did, get into the "business" which was often inherited by the children of the founder.

[2]When broadcast radio was still in its infancy, a local religious program was broadcast on Station KDKA in Pittsburgh. It was extremely successful, so much so, by 1925 at least 63 stations were owned outright by religious groups. In 1929 the Federal Communications Commission ruled that a fixed percentage of religious broadcast time was in the public interest and mandated a minimum time to be allotted by station licensees to religious programming—*free of charge*—in addition to any paid time. It turned out to be one of the FCC's most historic decisions. The ruling is still operative today. It was the birth of the electronic churches.

[14]The advent of the radio churches further, and even more dramatically, changed both institutional and evangelical religion. Tent show preaching was very impersonal, but radio preaching became downright remote, and so religious service had taken another, and very large, step away from religious tradition. Radio broadcasts were even more expensive than tent shows, and far more risky. A live attendee was a captive audience while a radio audience could leave anonymously with the twist of a dial. Still, in spite of the learning curve, it was only the beginning of electronic religion. The few who persevered soon learned they needed precisely the same skills as commercial programming in order to compete effectively. Audience participation services similar to Nielson and Arbitron were either hired or contracted. The productions became much more sophisticated and more national in scope. With radio, the audience could grow to millions from hundreds. Broadcast costs increased, but donations increased even more. But both the risks and the costs of this new media became quickly apparent, so much so in fact, most of the initial religious stations were out of business by 1930.

[2]Radio religion still wasn't the end of this technological makeover. In the late twenties, a new type of radio transmission was exhibited by an electronic engineer named Armstrong. He actually broadcast moving pictures along with synchronous sound. As popular as they were, radio religious services were a voice coming from a box. Although many of the radio preachers were well programmed and good performers, their audiences needed to reach into their own

personal resources to fill in the emotional blanks left by the faceless "voice from the box". By the 1950s, television became widespread, and television added the missing face. While there was still a physical disconnect between the preachers and their audiences, the television preachers became familiar, and the acquaintance was enhanced by the comfort of the home.

[2]The physical appearance and antics of the television preacher again became a significant factor in his success as it had in the earlier success of tent show preachers. The program organization, the scenery, the buildings, the decorations, even the staff and the audience itself, all acquired vital importance. Programs had to fit into time slots to harmonize with FCC commercial programming requirements. Plot lines had to be complete within those time slots. Even major story lines had rigid time constrictions in order to be serialized if necessary. Nielson type audience services became crucial not merely to check audience size, but to test audience response to story lines, formats, guests, and even to personalities. The program packages, were entirely market driven. The most successful performers, like Falwell, Robertson, and Schuller, actually developed their own in-house marketing facility. The content itself was enormously affected. Story lines which were perfectly acceptable in a conventional church setting, such as sexually suggestive Biblical recitations, became totally unacceptable in the television format. Story lines which were too long for the time slot, or visually wrong for the television media, or even contentious, had to be avoided. It might have been Marshall McCluan who early recognized the media as the story but broadcast religion recognized that wisdom before he did.

[7]There was an additional important factor in this market. Religious broadcasts were primarily paid for by contributions. Broadcasts which attempted to obtain sponsorship had to demonstrate both audience and response. The magic time for response, both by tradition and by participation, was Sunday morning. The narrow window of opportunity forced preaching into a competition which even aggressive revivalism had never before seen. Competition required organization, planning, finances, and technical specializations such as *no* religion had ever seen before. [2]Programs had to appear to be Bible associated and therefore, somehow, familiar, but not repetitive. To accomplish the purpose, program producers had to engage every technique known to commercial film and TV including voice-overs, zooms, music, volume changes, and all the others. Each program was carefully edited to fit a carefully analyzed audience. The production mode was determined and the treatment decided. The budget was meticulously planned. Production involved writers, directors, lighting, artists, camera specialists, casting, rehearsals, editing, syndication, sales and marketing. It particularly

incorporated financial appeals. Religious broadcasting had to become so commercial some of the TV preachers began presenting themselves as "talk show hosts", even appearing on commercial talk shows.

[16]And now, a new media is becoming widespread that will once again change the practice of religion, but this time on a global basis. In spite of their phenomenal accomplishment, the electronic churches had operational problems which were difficult to overcome. One of the big ones was FCC time slot limitations, and competition for a slot. Another one was measuring audience size and response. Still another one was collecting donations. The television churches will undoubtedly continue to prosper but Web site churches will expand audiences all over the world because they are inexpensive to establish, and because there are dissatisfied people of like mind all over the world. Now they can find each other on the Internet, almost regardless of location. There are no time slot limitations, and the FCC regulations play no part in this media. The Internet makes audience ("hit") count automatically. Donations can be sent instantly and the donation comes with a return Internet address which is automatically added to subscriber lists for future reference. With the addition of digital motion pictures becoming more common, chat rooms can go television one better by being interactive. All of this can substantially contribute to the viability of cyber churches which compete with the establishment and video churches.

While it is difficult to envision cyber churches ever substituting for television congregations, seventy five years ago few would have dared to predict television churches competing with conventional churches as they do today. Digital technology has modified methods and loyalties, but most fundamentally, it has altered patterns and perceptions forever. This era is growing in the (exaggerated) social frame of mind that technology is a universal key and religious congregations based on such a mindset appear to fit within the construction. [4][7]Conventional churches are reaching into cyber technology, which is symptomatic of their recognition that religious people increasingly want a more individually meaningful "connection" to God. For many observant the great institutions are more ritualistic than religious and in that regard, at least, the wanderers are responding to an age of unmediated personal access. Television churches as well are making attempts to tap into the "ad hoc" religious communities by means of Web site outreach in an obvious effort to meet the Internet competition on its own ground. Internet denominations have a visceral fear of Vatican-like centralism much as did the video churches from which most of the online churches evolved. Modern communication technology is their best palliative so it is probable modem cyber churches will become a common phenomenon, and it will doubtless produce the same content disparity with the original message as had the prior broadcast rendering. With all the deviant practice and content, cyber churches are here to stay.

[19]Splintering is not by any means restricted to the Protestant community. The Jewish community of the millennium is splintering even more deeply. Under external attack for several millenniums, Jews had previously presented a unified visage to the outside world. At the beginning of the twentieth century, most of the Jews arriving in America were escaping the confining ghettos of east European cities. When they made the frightening decision to emigrate to America, most of them did it with vengeance; leaving almost everything behind including their religion but notably, not their culture. As much as 80% of the new arrivals were secular but profoundly "Jewish". They found widespread communal anti-Semitism in the United States, but relatively little institutional restriction. The Jews organized their own schools, unions, professional organizations, and even communities. They learned from millenniums of sad experience, their chances of overcoming obstacles improved with a form of unity which sometimes approached the brink of xenophobia, and with that strategy, they submerged all their much storied differences.

The one nation in which earned their unrestrained ethnic loyalty was the United States because here, for the first time in several thousand years, they felt relatively safe. This attitude was so globally widespread Stalin was convinced all Russian Jews were potential American spies. His paranoia actually had some basis. Virtually every Russian Jew had relatives in America. So it is almost sardonic that America turned out to be the straw that broke the back of Jewish unity. [5]As fear was the glue of Jewish unity, so was safety its solvent. For several thousand years, their common destiny was undifferentiated by their individual divergences. In America, finally, the group fate started to divide.

[5]Historically, Judaism and Jewishness were two very distinct forces, one being religious and the other cultural and usually secular. Identifying the religion was easy but the culture was much more complex because it was always a mix of the ancient core with the dominant outside culture, be that German, French, Polish, Russian, American, or whatever. The dominant "Jewish" language was not Hebrew. It was "Yiddish". Nobody raised the question of who was Jewish because the secular Jews lived among other Jews immersed in Jewish culture—and they, the secular, were the majority of American Jews. After World War II, they Americanized and started to move away from those communities, lose the ties of culture, and even intermarry.

Unlike the Christians, who could research their individual genealogies, the Jews, largely thanks to several thousand years of massacres and migrations could only recreate their religious derivations. The slim thread which tied them to their own history began to fray. Religion offered a handle and a return to community as well, but as secularism faded, it was replaced with a kind of religious diversity which the American diversity itself fed. [19]There were Orthodox groups, and Conservative groups, and Reform groups, and Labor Zionist groups, and Hasidic groups, and many others, as well as many ongoing secular groups. The different assemblies began to fragment along political lines as well as religious. The ancient Jewish unity fractured badly along doctrinal religious differences, and now, like American Protestants, along political fault lines which, only a few years before, would never have surfaced. There is the story of a rescue mission that locates a lone Jewish man marooned on a deserted island for many years. To their surprise, they find two synagogues on the island. Of course they ask why he needed two synagogues. "Well, the one over there", he answers, "is the one I never attend". Arguments about what was Jewish tradition, what was local custom, and what was essentially religious mandate broke out. And eventually, those differences became sharp enough to trigger a debate of "who was Jewish?"

They were not academic arguments. For Jews, the "melting pot" had worked". During all the years in Europe intermarriage had been unusual but not unknown. In post World War II America, intermarriage had reached over 51% which meant Jews marrying Jews were actually the exception and their children, for the most part, were not choosing to be Jews! Furthermore, each division of Judaism, and to some extent, each geography of Judaism has its own conversion rules, and questions the other's legitimacy. [19]As a matter of fact, they don't even recognize variant rabbis as legitimate so conversions must be tested for both the convert and for his rabbi. For the Israelis, for example, where their Arab population is already growing faster than their Jewish population, the implications must be very seriously weighed. Orthodox Israelis did not recognize American marriages much less their conversions. Those are the same Americans who are Israel's major political and financial supporter. (Just as an aside, it is important to recall Israel was established as a specifically secular democracy, in fact, the only nation of either description in the Middle-East.)

American education was motivated by diversity but orthodoxy bans women's direct participation in religious services, education in religious matters, or even confirmation as Jews. Indeed, orthodoxy even prohibits their passively sitting with men during those services. Today Jewish women are perhaps the most educated and upwardly mobile identifiable group in either the United States or in

Israel and they are achieving recognition and rewards in every profession from astronomy to zoology, inclusive. It is a very rare Jewish woman who does not own or operate a computer and almost unique for such a person not to have access to the internet. They drive. They use cell phones. They run companies. And, equally important, they balance their own check books. Working mothers are more the rule than the exception, and those working mothers are vital to the survival of the family and the Jewish ethic. To tell women who have achieved professional and financial status in an era of revolutionary technology they are not allowed, or perhaps not qualified, to participate in the religious process, is obviously going to take some serious reconsideration in the millennium.

[7]And so, unlike Evangelical Christianity, the millennial problem of Judaism is not the technology which permits outreach to others. Rather, for the Jews it is the same technology which encourages inreach from which they were previously shielded. Among the Jews themselves, religiosity seems to have won the battle with secularism. They would appear to have won their ancient battle for ecumenism, which they have demanded since the origins of the Common Era. [19]That self same victory might become the greatest millennial hazard to their community identification. Before the modern global technocracy, few Jews ever asked "Who is a Jew?" The slogan of the United Jewish Appeal has been "We Are One". The Israeli parliament unanimously passed a mandate known as the "Law of Return" which guaranteed the unconditional right to immigrate to Israel to all Jews of any stripe, from any land of origin. It was a universal reaction to history, recent and ancient. If the Jewish people themselves can not reach a consensus on what is a Jew, it will have ramifications for the millennial American community scene, Jew and Christian alike.

[9]Islam is in the headlines in one way or another every single day. In the West, there was clearly general, if uneven economic improvement. It is hard to argue the proposition that technology has brought benefits. Not so the Moslem nations which are among the poorest of the poor. However, for all, rich and poor alike, the era has brought communications. Muslims everywhere have become aware of people's progress elsewhere, progress which they don't themselves share. Since the defeat of the Ottoman Empire the world has been largely dominated by those Western nations either politically, economically, or both, so blaming the West for their quandary is easy and to some extent, factual. (Of course, one might observe in passing Islam progressed in reverse under the Muslim Ottomans as well.) Just as Protestantism, during the reformation, became the vehicle of European yearning, so has Islam become the Moslem agency of resistance during the current era.

Islam is a growing segment of the American religious community. It comes from many different areas of the globe, notably Africa, the Middle-East, and Asia. For Islam that is a problem. At least initially, American religions were fragmented along national lines, because most of them came from Europe. Islam is geographically segmented with ancient tribal hostilities in addition to the many national conflicts. Even within the tribes, clan warfare separated people. Indeed, many historians believe peace among the tribes was the Prophet's core message. Practices, and even attitudes, among the new American Islamic communities are so severely differentiated there is little, if any, contact between those congregations beyond the common reference to the Koran. There is probably more intermarriage between American Islamic and non-Islamic people, than there is between Islamic people of different ethnic backgrounds so their first challenge in the millennium will be to develop an Islamic melting pot in America before they produce an Islamic-American melting pot. It is almost fair to say there is no national "Islamic community" in America at the turn of the millennium.

[1][15]With so many new arrivals of the faith, they experience a new kind of problem, that of minority status. Some see interaction with non-Muslims as a violation of the faith. The great immigrant fear of "interaction" is absorption—i.e., accepting the values and behavior of the host culture. For this group, the twenty-first century will be first and foremost one of establishing their Islamic independent identity in the midst of the dominant host while simultaneously disassociating themselves from the extremism of a very visible Islamic minority. It is not an experience unique to Moslems but it's not easy to do. Their children will appear in greater and greater numbers in the public schools where isolation is not only discouraged, it is impossible. American schools have always served as the vehicle of integration. Jobs, politics, entertainment and even food will ultimately change their past lifestyles. Even the reality of a secular government will pose some difficulties for a cultural group for whom government and religion were synonymous.

[7][13]But perhaps the most fateful impact of millennial America on immigrants will be the position of women. In the Muslim nations, the rights of women are severely limited to an extent, in some areas, approaching outright slavery. In most of those places, women had no choices, and no knowledge of choices. In America, such circumstance will dispel immediately. Citizenship, voting rights, dress codes, access to education, family planning, divorce, and shopping, will all strongly influence their behavior. It is the "Women's Lib" that many of the orthodox nations are most worried about, and in America, such concerns will very likely be demonstrated as valid. Legally enforced access to education is,

as in the case of Jews, access to opportunity and equality. It is also access to a technology which is changing the world.

[13]Further complicating their problem is another peculiarity of American history. The recent movement of immigrants to the Americas is not the first Islamic wave to reach our shores. It has been estimated that as much as 40% of the victims of African American slavery were originally Islamic and they have been here longer than most of the Europeans. Many converted to Christianity during the period of slavery, and some reverted to Islam after the Civil War. Many, perhaps most, of the recent "reverts" such as Mohammed Ali, are Americans of African descent trying to "re-root", as are so many others at this time of losing heritage. In any case, newcomers arriving on our shores must somehow deal not only with disparate Muslim communities from several continents (contrary to popular impression, less than 15% of American Muslims are of Middle-Eastern origin), but with an indigenous American community as well, with whom their community contact is virtually zero. It is fascinating to realize that one of the questions of the millennium is "Who is a Jew?" But, another one of the upcoming questions for Islam might be "Who is a Muslim?"

Their tribal past had been used to hold back the world in their native countries but in the Information Age, such strategems is now failing everywhere. The vaunted notion of defending "the faith" might have had some semblance of verity in a time when the Sahara Desert separated people, but when camel drivers use cell phones to call their relatives in America, the tribal obsession with "us" and "them" might not sell as well. Whoever the target of the moment is, the Muslim terrorist's ultimate mark is their own people. [12]The greatest threat to orthodoxy is their own women, more illiterate than the men and even more repressed and restless. Women's shops in Saudi Arabia are actually banned, but the hottest underground market is sexy lingerie purchased by women. Women are much less invested in orthodoxy because they are its victims. A greater threat than women in general, are the American educated women in particular, who are beginning to demand more access to the levers of power, education, jobs, and freedom. It is not without reason the Afghan Imams didn't allow women out on the street. In this regard, America is a particularly dangerous adversary.

[13]In fundamentalist countries, women achieve literacy at enormous personal risk of life and freedom. They must obey the laws of the Koran as interpreted through men. In direct contrast, American law requires universal education which then allows women to read the Koran themselves and the reading is markedly different from the interpretation they were exposed to. [12]They are demanding and acquiring educations not only in Koran, but in professions,

and history, and social studies, and driving, and money management. They are developing women's schools, services, and clinics which, incidentally, include marriage and abuse counseling—unheard of in their previous experience. Muslim women raised in America are upwardly mobile for the first time in history and will begin transmitting all of this back to their relatives in the old country. Computers and the Internet, in those countries, are slow in coming because of repression and illiteracy, but even there, multi-function cell phones are becoming available and the computers are not far behind. Time and tide are changing Islamic fundamentalism and it is very likely, in this millennium, the women will turn the global tectonic rumblings under the feet of orthodox Muslims, and perhaps orthodox Jews and Christians as well, into earthquakes. Given the level of exodus from their nations, it is very likely the "Judeo-Christian" designation so common to our public pronouncements in America will be modified to "Judeo-Christian-Islamic".

Secularism (Oxford English Dictionary) is a philosophy which supports the exclusion of all considerations drawn from belief in God from governmental process in a society, but not from the private lives of the citizens. [7]Secularists are not necessarily atheists. In that definition, the founding fathers of the United States included many secularists. Many theologians actually support secularism because they favor the idea of a wall isolating any government from support of any form of religious activity. It is an attitude which, in the age of information, actually does have attractions. Most of the subject matter of this volume is the visible results of separation of church and science. Not often included in discussions of religion, "Secularism" is not new. For most societies in history where church attendance was not mandatory, the attendees were a minority. Even Victorian England, where attendance was sometimes actually taken, usually only showed about a 33% attendance record. The rise of science might be expected to be something of a counterweight to the increase in religious participation. The perspectives of science appear to support rewards which are the apparent outcome of human efforts rather than any non-natural intervention. Diseases will be reduced to a greater extent. Food will become more abundant. More jobs will have been created. Life will continue to be improved. And even now when the third world needs help, they don't go to the church. They are more likely to apply to the International Relief Agencies.

One would expect, in such a context, secular political expression would increase. While Europe, perhaps in the aftermath of the holocaust and the post war invasion of their very diverse former colonial immigrants, is more secular, this is not the case for the American scene. America appears to be shopping for a more democratic religion, one perhaps, more suited to the new age of technology. It might be reasonable to conclude the early rise of secularism was an indication of the failure of religion, but if that is so, then the current rebirth of religion would be evidence of the failure of secularism. Remarkably, religion has always been one of the threads which stitched our secular society together. [7]Sir Julian Huxley declared a hundred years ago "what the world needs is not merely a denial of the old, but an affirmation of the new". If he was right, the secularists are in for as much change in this new age as people of faith.

The "religion" aspect of this volume would not be complete without some discussion of technology itself as a kind of millennial salvation belief. For science, the driving energy of our age, no observable event is mystical. At a time when no event is "unnatural", the nature of "nature" is being defined as never before in history. Scientists are not only describing the character of the present universe, their theoretical contemplations are going back to the very first instant of creation. Scientists are making very viable experimental confirmations of their mathematic speculations. (Technology always demands repeatable demonstration.) It is not based on any ultimate truth but rather on continually refined and corrected clarifications. Therefore, change is inherent in technology and in that sense it sets the mode of the times.

[16]With science changing the lives and attitudes of the world, many conclude knowledge is providing all the answers missing from other creeds. It would certainly appear logical, but it probably won't fly. The ultimate language of science is mathematics. One plus one must equal two, else back to the drawing boards. Even in the millennium, and particularly in this new culture, two people will always have the potential for three opinions. Emotions are not mathematical and if there is any lesson to be gleaned from the bloody dictatorships of the 1900s, the instruction should be that peoples' individual needs and behaviors can't be predicated on a mathematical basis. Millennial science will not become a viable substitute for religion for the very qualities of personal choice science itself is enhancing. Indeed, institutional religions are under coercion for those very same reasons. The "nature" of nature is impersonal. Where the subject of morality begins to show dimension, science has no numbers, no mystique, and makes no effort to provide "transcendent truths". It can provide the bread of life, but, as has long been recognized, man does not live by bread alone. People will continue to derive their most visceral satisfactions from the exultation of human relationships, and as long as it remains true, faith will occupy its separate space. Science, even in this millennial age of science, will not likely offset such a universal need and it is one feature which the "information age" probably won't change.

Organized denominational religions—all of them, including Christian, Jewish, and Islamic—are at the same crossroads at the onset of the twenty-first century much as the Catholic religion was at the onset of the 16th, and for much the same reasons. European people, their commerce and their industrial culture were spreading around the world. The Catholic Church's options were to bend or break. At that time their perception was that bending would be equivalent to breaking so they made the wrong decision and the supremacy of Catholicism in Western Europe ended. Now all the breakaway religions of the Reformation are at the same juncture. It is intriguing that in this millennium, the battle for the "Rock of Ages" may be resolved by the technology of the age of rocks.

Aside from all of their differences of doctrine, American religions have some very common problems directly attributable to modern technology. Religion is a very personal commitment but in the information age, small abstract differences become ideological issues if a fellowship can be found. Modern technology facilitates fellowship location and those ideological associates need no longer be in the same place, with familiar people, or even on the same continent. An ancient platitude praises the pleasures of "brothers dwelling together". That is the way it always was but it won't necessarily be that way any more. In the context of the much famed "information explosion", factors such as job migration will substitute for personal factors in homesteading choices. It will force people to choose between financial security, and religious familiarity. Whichever is the winner, the residue will inevitably do damage to time hallowed practice and many cozy attitudes. Dispersion into a disparate society encourages competition of ideas, and it virtually forces adaptation as well. Even if faithfulness prevails, "faithfulness to what?" will become a major subject of debate and of conscience in this oncoming age.

The ubiquitous harvest of technology is choices and changes. As technology spreads and deepens, more people will have more alternatives. All the institutions of everyday life, the religious institutions no less than any others, will offer a growing menu of more personalized alternatives. All the religions will make serious and painful accommodations to a very dynamic age of demystification and of scientific enquiry. Religious institutions will be forced to compete with more personalized versions outside of those institutions. It is very comfy to think of an enduring "Church" but none of our forefathers would recognize its' modern practice.

Summary:

In the age of a global market economy where product choices will be clamorously available, and where the technologies will make those choices ever more compelling, intractably rigid religions will be losing ground to the more individually tailored faiths. The Methodists, the Lutherans, the Presbyterians, the Episcopalians, and even the Holy Roman church have all already been impacted by the process and are being forced by logistics to modify their message and their target audiences. [16]For example, Catholics are losing their previously "locked in" Hispanic audience to churches like the Pentecostals. They are also losing their teaching staff. [17]In 1965, more than 4,000 women entered their religious orders and less than 500 left. Five years later, less than 700 entered but more than 2000 left. [8]In 1958, less than 5% of churchgoers had changed faith. By 1985, the figure was over 25%. All the religions will become "market oriented" or they will suffer serious losses of market share.

Not only will the message be revamped for that purpose, but delivery as well. All the religions, including the most traditional institutions, will be forced to enlarge on electronic network church operations and even include Internet Web sites, CD ROMS, and potentially risky chat rooms—hazardous because they can include interfaith participants with contrasting viewpoints. Reflecting the same condition, Internet and Cable religious programs will reach more and more diverse people. The National Interfaith Cable Coalition already purportedly represents over 65 individual religious groups with no ruling determination of overall attitudes or needs.

It is only the beginning. The millennial changes in practice of all the world's faiths are unquestionably going to be as extensive as is every other aspect of the era. At the turn of the millennium, many of those changes are already quite evident. For instance, many religious institutions are forming "partnerships" with niche groups like ethnic, and racial, and activist fringe assemblies crossing hitherto impassable divides. The Mormon Church was traditionally white, but many of their new converts are non-white. The Catholic Church is evolving charismatic type "prayer meetings". Even the remaining faithful are making adaptations to local conditions, "Liberation Theology" being an obvious example. Orthodox Jewish women are forming women's prayer "clubs". Inter-denominational associations like "Habitat for Humanity" and "Promise Keepers" are sprouting everywhere for every designated reason. These new associations are being actively aided and abetted by the connectivity of a world dominated by Internet, multi-function cell phones, PDA's and an incoming blizzard of non-denominational association routes.

Structural variation is also germinating. Millennial religions will probably become more impersonal in terms of pastoral relationships, but more individual in terms of practice. They will almost certainly be less managed as witness the lay Catholic revolt against their Bishop's decisions regarding child abuse by priests—a striking illustration of growing demand for more local control. Another is the special interest ministries which compete with national ministries. The local ministries are much more likely to form issue based ecumenical associations such as immigrant rights, abortion rights, civil rights, home schooling, and even liturgical attitudes as between Catholic, Anglican, and Eastern Orthodox congregations. Experience demonstrates the local religious groups are more likely to associate spiritual with social needs and affiliate with those of like mind but not necessarily of like theology. Needless to say there will be no shortage of issues to aggregate around.

Those kinds of interfaith associations will certainly amplify the probability of sharing facilities, an outcome warranted by the inevitability of uncertain finances consequent to unstable congregations. Such considerations have raised issues never before considered by the religious community in America. The prospect of government supported church social services such as soup kitchens, drug rehab centers, employment counseling, job training, child care centers, marriage counseling, and even medical services such as flu shots, etc., appeared as one solution but it will raise some very legitimate concerns on both sides of this approach. Many such services are, in fact, more effective when combined with religious training. Presuming the assumption to be true, should the fear of proselytizing override the best interests of the client? Should the government subsidize such services for non-mainstream religions? Remembering most modern religious variations were once a break-away, how does the government distinguish between mainstream and unique faiths or between religions and cults? On the other hand, many religions are understandably concerned that government subsidies would ultimately imply government control of message and method.

Furthermore, the conceivable government-sponsored growth of such "not for profit" local church services as soup kitchens, store front churches, charities, and so on, will pose problems for the community in which they locate. They will reduce the tax base directly because they are tax exempt, while increasing tax rates indirectly because they reduce property values, require more services, and introduce more parking lots, traffic and noise. Charities of almost any kind often bring people to the neighborhoods who might be considered non-local at best and undesirable at worst. For the elderly and parents of children, this is not necessarily a mean spirited concern.

In this oncoming time of swift and probably accelerating passage, historic norms will constantly be weighed against current needs. Pieties will often be heard from charlatans or even worse, from ministers who claim vision but are so clueless as to preach by poll. People will be searching for lifetime footings. In such a quest many are already turning to religion as their anchor. They might find solace but it is unlikely they will find constancy. Religion in the information age will be being motivated into a global venue with a wider variation of faiths and customs and acquire practices very novel to popular memory.

All the churches of the millennium are going to have some really new clerical accessories which will include media offices with fax, computer and modem equipment, chat lines and Web sites. They will need to hire full time media specialists and make media literacy a requirement for all their top level functionaries including the ministers. That will probably mean that courses in English literacy and media science will be mandatory for theology schools. As never before, the business of America has truly become business, and the churches, mainline and on-line, will be no exceptions, with more technology and more consumerism. The competition will be fierce.

The control of mainline religions will probably be forced to decentralize ever further. That in turn means a more democratized, individualized structure of faiths very likely to be "anti-intellectual", i.e., anti-educationally biased at a time when education is virtually the only route to economic progress. These more democratic religious institutions of the millennium will face the potentiality of increasing anarchy of message in a society which is itself rapidly diversifying. The reaction could be a very reckless fundamentalism which might be, in the dynamics of the twenty-first century, be more destabilizing than the diversity.

Fundamentalism itself will be more conflicted. America is a nation which basically accepts the separation of church and state and the most orthodox of believers, save for a very few, are not proposing to modify the tradition. Even those who would like to see more religious subject matter in classrooms and Congress overwhelmingly do not support enabling legislation which would underwrite that outcome. Many, perhaps most, non-Muslim new arrivals who came here of their own free choice, subconsciously came to avoid the ancient marriage of church and state as one of their major motivations. Arab immigrants, on the other hand, acquiesced to the partnership but were motivated to emigrate by economic hopelessness, without necessarily recognizing the association. For some, the secular state is not only a new experience, it is an immoral condition. [9]Fundamentalist

Islamic states see their mission as conversion of the world society, not revision of their own social order. The extremists may be a minority in their own areas, but the troubles they generate will echo around the world producing problems and at least some resonance for Muslims everywhere. Often, it is those with the least stake in the past who defend antiquity most actively for fear of losing identity, virtually their only possession. Technology such as the Internet, makes it very easy for them to find each other.

Many early sociologists forecast the diminution of organized religion as a growing trend of the time. They turned out to be very wrong. One century later, religious faith is obviously alive and doing well in the American community but it is equally clear that there are going to be some big winners and very big losers in the twenty-first. Millennial model churches, being relatively recently arrived on the American scene, seem to fit better with a modern industrial technological age of individual needs and goals, personal achievement, and an inescapably mobile lifestyle. New churches are constructed around such a paradigm. Main-line churches are deconstructing centuries of tradition in order to rebuild in a modern mode. In the West, this is a familiar, although painful process. The "traditional" churches have always changed or they probably would not have survived. This time, however, the adjustments will be far more wrenching and over a much shorter time lapse. They will need to change their leadership, their organization, and their message. It is going to be a difficult time for conformity.

Reading and Reference:

[1] *A History of God*, Karen Armstrong ISBN 0 345 38456 3

[2] *Televangelism*, Razelle Frankl ISBN 0 8093 1299 9

[3] *The Road of Science and the Ways to God* S.L.Jaki ISBN 0 226 39144 2

[4] the *Atlantic Monthly* Opening of the Evangelical Mind Alan Wolf

[5] *Jew vs. Jew* S.G.Freedman ISBN 0 684 85944 0

[6] *SoulTsunami* Leonard Sweet ISBN 0 310 22762-3

[7] *Religion and Change* D.L.Edwards

[8] *Shopping for Faith* Cimino & Lattin ISBN 0 7879 4170 0

[9] *Islam and Democracy* Fatima Mernissi ISBN 0-201-62483-4

[10] *Islamic Fundamentalism*. Mohammad Mohaddessin

[11] *Islam in America*. Phylis Lan Lin

[12] *Islam, Liberty and Development* Mohammad Khatami

[13] *American Muslims* Hasan

[14] *Reinventing American Protestantism* Miller ISBN 0 520 20938 9

[15] *The Battle for God* Karen Armstrong 0 345 39169 1

[16] *Give Me That Online Religion* B.E. Brasher 0 7879 4579 X

[17] *Newsweek* January 1, 2000

[18] *The Economist* December 21, 2002

[19] *Real Jews* N.J.Efron 0 465 01854 8

3

Community—The Slipping Mooring

[2]Most towns have traditionally been built around industries and transportation. Many towns, like Detroit, were actually built around factories. That is already, at the beginning of the twenty-first century, a vestigial remnant of another time. Plants can be assembled almost anywhere and disassembled even faster, depending more on politics than on geography. All that is needed are the communication links to remotely operate the plant and they can be installed almost overnight. The "Bells" (big and little), Motorola, AT&T, Nextel, and Verizon, to mention only a few illustrations, have, between them many satellites, and many more towers going operational almost routinely. Within twenty five years, the majority of U.S. workers will be information workers who use such links. They will not necessarily work in factories or offices. Their inputs will be manipulated by computers over cell phones, palm pilots, and the many other devices just coming on market along with the satellites, cables, fiber optic telephone lines, and even the twentieth century anachronism, radio.

Even aside from remote factories, those same installations affect Main Street directly. The "meter man", i.e., people who come around every month to read water, gas, electric, and any other utility usage are as vestigial as the company town. All of it will be, and in fact is already, being done remotely and automatically. Indeed, the billing itself will be executed and delivered electronically so even the letter postal services are losing ground.

[4]Electronic information processing has become so commonplace virtually every library catalog is already on line. Not only can reservations for books be made on line but (I'm personally very sorry to see this.) the books themselves are increasingly on line. In a period of such dramatic conversion, local newspapers are obviously struggling to keep pace with TV and metropolitan papers. Both of those as well are losing ground to the on-line computer sources where you can lit-

erally construct a newspaper tailored to your own taste from daily articles published all over the world, and have it delivered every day, usually with no charge. "Help wanted" and "job wanted" ad's are now being placed via the internet and some agencies are actually substituting terminals for agents to service clients who lack internet availability elsewhere. As a matter of fact, some employment agencies are considering installing dedicated public computer terminals like ATMs in key areas. All of this changes the way life is lived in any community. All of it reduces the disparities of lifestyle and opportunity between small and large communities. Large revisions in city planning and services will become mandated by the demands of the new Main Street, in part because most of the new life style is triggered by and facilitated by new technology.

[2]In a background in which energy and environmental concerns will make good politics, land use commissions will be forced to review and revise attitudes to adapt to the changes and that isn't new. Working at home blends well with the growing social imperative of reducing the use of automobiles. Interestingly, home offices also add to the stability of communities in an age of employment instability since information workers won't necessarily change their location every time they change jobs. In addition to reducing road usage, home offices increase the incentive to invest in homes which could be a long term residences. The investment would include extra home insulation, more efficient smart heating and cooling systems, down to "smart" dishwashers and laundry machines operating during minimum demand hours. Technologically updating homes, in contrast to merely cosmetic improvements, will have the obvious consequence of increasing house value (and tax assessments).

[8] Home offices will have been designed for "fold-away" utility so that the "office" furniture will be out of sight when not in use, much like the famous "Murphy" beds. In fact, because of the possibility increased worker mobility, even the office type home designs will be smaller than current homes so a return of "Murphy" layouts is highly probable. Modems will probably be built into the home network system with different computers in different parts of the house able to talk to each other and to the Internet as well. This is already a recognized market with many companies such as Intel, Nortel, Motorola, Lucent Cisco, IBM, Panasonic, and others producing the equipment and several producing equipment in more than one medium. Some take the form of accessories that use the electric wiring as the carrier connection within the house so little if any modification is necessary. Others use short range wireless.

[5]Some of the new advances will necessitate radical changes in construction codes and materials. Multi-purpose cable inter-connects for computer network-

ing (LAN) and remote control is one such code modification on the horizon. Another one is home lighting. [9][10][19]Tungsten light bulbs and even fluorescent tubes are very soon going to be the dinosaurs of home lighting. In terms of efficiency, only five percent of their tungsten bulb energy input turns up as light. Ninety five percent is wasted as heat. LEDs (Light Emitting Diodes) are far more efficient because they generate virtually no heat. Automobile dashboards, alarms, calculators, meters, etc., are very common current applications because of their low energy usage. The previous home lighting LED quandary was producing white light, but no more. It is anticipated that further development will produce LEDs which emit ten times as much light per watt as a tungsten bulb. Cost competitive white lights composed of LED assemblies are now in very active development on three continents. The new assemblies in progress are extremely energy efficient, have an operating lifetime anticipated to be in the tens of thousands of hours (their useful lifetimes will approach the market lifetime of a typical home), produce almost no heat, and most interesting, are flat plates constructed as part of room walls, invisible when not in use. They will eliminate light fixtures, and, very likely, eliminate many manufacturers in the bulb business. White LED lighting is already being used in traffic signaling, retail displays, walkway illumination, special stage lighting, emergency lights, and many other applications—just by way of demonstrating that this is fast becoming a widespread device. What makes this device so fascinating is that for the very first time, home lighting can potentially become "central" in exactly the same way home heating became central. With a single light source in the house, light energy can be conveyed throughout the home by means of fiber optics (itself becoming a mature technology) and manually or automatically "turned on" in the local room area where human presence is sensed. Aside from the intrinsic high energy efficiency of LED lighting, the additional efficiency produced by a central lighting source will very quickly overcome initial installation costs.

[10]Lighting being such a basic, code revision will be motivated but this will also encourage, if not force, the inclusion of higher value components such as computers, sensors, controllers, transponders, lighting controls, built in entertainment and communication and energy management as part of the building structure rather than as accessories. This kind of advanced "construction material" will eliminate the distinction between technology and housing. Construction codes will be modified to embrace lighting as a structural material, and a host of other new concepts. High tech material will need to be maintained and repaired conveniently and economically so they will likely be modular in nature, i.e., removable and replaceable rather than repairable, and will undoubtedly

become as regulated as all the other material construction codes. As energy sources begin to reflect reality, construction codes will begin to include alternative energy considerations.

With the proper identification such as you have on a bankcard, all utilities will be able to be controlled from locations remote from the house (or office). [5][8]There are already over twenty million American homes with more than one computer in them and in passing, there are over one half million homes with home network wiring already built into them. It doesn't seem like many except in perspective. Three years ago there were less than fifty thousand such homes. Those computers will be controlling the appliances, the lighting, the air conditioning, the water systems, TV, telephones, and even security equipment. Home networking (included as Local Area Networking called "LAN") is already a spreading business with some real heavy weights like Panasonic, IBM, Motorola, as well as Lucent and Cisco putting their toes in the water—and those are only a few of the American firms working on this growing market. There are as many foreign firms doing development work. This would already be a larger market, one impediment being existing housing which will have to be modified to accommodate the new equipment. New houses in the near term will be built against home networking specifications much as gas lines and electric wiring became part of new home construction codes.

Easily convertible home-office type designs will still need to reflect human occupant personality and have the normal individual amenities which make life comfortable, to say nothing of livable. The ancient rectangular geometry so typical of our buildings, the lighting, fixed walls, single purpose rooms, will all give way to utilitarian shapes, indiscernible lighting, and controllably transparent walls. For the purpose of living space interchangeability, household utilities such as stoves, refrigerators, counters, sinks, and even equipment such as vacuum cleaners will need to be downsized and designed to be "stowed" during office hours. All the technology, computers, fax machines, etc., will need to "disappear" from sight when the hours of home life return, which again mandates a radically new approach to building construction, architecture, and municipal codes. Such a demand, as it grows will spawn new types of dual function utility and furniture industries because the home furnishing will tend to be "built in" which implies both more house to house conformity and permanence.

Much as the Industrial Revolution divorced the home from the job, the Information Revolution will at least tend to remarry them. With information workers becoming the bulk of the American working staff and many of them exercising the preference to work at home, community amenities will undergo great modifications. Working and living at the same location was unexceptional at turn of the twentieth century. Mom and Pop usually lived above "Mom and Pop" shops, many of which generated both noise and traffic. Automobiles in smaller towns and public transportation in larger ones allowed the increasing separation of career and home, but information age work generates neither noise nor traffic so any such zoning will and should become obsolete. As these job arrangements grow, along with changed zoning and construction regulations, the new circumstances will change the housing market in such regards as special wiring, digital cables, and fiber optics, all the way down to home office security including such considerations as special temperature control, emergency electrical supply, and privacy.

[6]Information workers in general and home office workers in particular, will tend to be better educated, more affluent, and probably more likely to be longer term residents. Factory workers will tend to be far more transient. The transient population, independent of income, would find it inappropriate to buy rather than rent housing since the costs of constantly closing old mortgages and opening new ones would be unwise even it were affordable. This will very likely encourage "house swapping" or a specialized version of "time shares" between regions. It implies an increasing degree of standard housing layouts so the swaps are equal and easy. This also implies two classes of people whose interests are separated by the *nature* of their occupation, not exclusively the remuneration. It means, as an example, the communities of the future will need to plan for trailer populations which are not just variable in terms of their identities, but in their absolute numbers, their service requirements, their schools, and their infrastructure needs as well. It also points to community planning differences that will need attention. Two income households will be more likely to "eat out", a pattern which must be built into the area zoning. Commercial shopping facilities will need to be very locally convenient. That is a reversal of the traditional zoning pattern of separation of residential and commercial. For multi-family high rise dwellings, it might even be necessary to build the shopping right into the building.

None of which even mentions the design distinctiveness needed to accommodate growing population segments with very unique needs. One of the serious revisions of modern medical research is the treatment of aging as a disease. The industry consensus of gerontology (aging) research supports great confidence that *average* life span is going to abruptly increase to well over one hundred years within the next two or three decades. (If this idyllic intention is realized, most retirees are going to run out of funds.) Divorce and single parenthood are growing apace. In addition it should come as no surprise that with over half the women already working after having children, the future will only increase their number. These women continue to provide the same chores to their families as their stay-at-home sisters so convenient multi-language schools are not abstract issues. And hardly least, work transience will produce unique needs different from those of the longer term population.

[6]From the perspective of any community, such a combination of circumstance implies a surge in multi-generational living arrangements. Building architecture as well as building codes will adapt to extensive demographic shift. Those distinctions are all likely to produce separated districts unless amenities are designed to bridge population divisions. Common facilities such as convenient day care, shopping, schools, safe walking, bicycling, and play areas will need to be planned in order for the towns of the future to be cohesive. Social infrastructure will also tend to contain the online trend toward isolation of people from their neighborhood. The evolving task of city planning will be to connect those sharply diverse populations.

[25]Shopping malls and stores themselves are going to undergo great alteration. Both will probably begin to resemble show rooms rather than present day shops, in order to compete with online shopping, carrying little or no inventory. Lack of inventory provides online "shops" with a financial advantage sufficiently large as to render most local shops non-competitive. Eventually the local shops might actually become the display room and warehouses for the online shops paying them, as it were, a commission for successful referrals. In order to compete as this scenario develops, and it will, independent shops will consist of a hybrid of "sample" wares and electronic cataloging. There will always be "better shops" that actually carry inventory to be "tried on" but the difference will be reflected on the price tag. Since the electronic catalog aspect can be viewed in the privacy of the home, malls will begin to expand secondary sales functions, much as book shops are becoming "reading rooms", in order to attract clientele. Therefore, Malls as well will need built in construction innovations such as private booths, keyboards, screens, search systems, three dimensional presentations, etc. And this too will need expanded, certainly differentiated, construction requirements.

[4]Further complicating the mix, the new reality will even include psychologically novel hurdles as well. For example, the home worker's largest contact with "the office" will be via a screen. Some, perhaps many, might not personally *know* any of their corporate colleagues. At the same time, they will "know" their immediate families on a twenty four hour, seven day a week basis. It's a condition of isolation not generally experienced for more than one hundred years. Individual remoteness such as the much fabled nineteenth century Wild West made for

some great stories but a terrible life style, and one which would not work today. With all the possibly enhanced quality family relationships, the non-family connectivity of what Alvin Toffler calls the "telecommunity" is not nearly the equivalent of a real handshake. Practical communal configuration of the twenty first century will go beyond building social centers where people can play cards. Libraries, cultural activities, broad student spectrum educational facilities, and probably public Internet access will all support mingling among neighbors. Communities have been commonly described as "networks of individuals" which were usually linked to "place". In the telecommunity, place, like jobs, will be evanescent. "Contacts" will be more important than ever for the purpose of finding those jobs. Research has, in fact, demonstrated the more successful an individual is in his professional life, the greater the scale of his "associations". That is specifically what will need re-establishment in the age of "telecommunities". A very basic demand will be to find innovative and original ways to create a human society which provides the professional and personal satisfactions of proximate groups and yet is essentially independent of geography. It will be a very tall order because associations are very fragile.

These are not really newly-arrived ideas. Back near the middle of the nineteenth century a German steel company named Krupp began to build living quarters for its workers for very good reasons. Through all the wars of that turbulent era, Krupp was well on its way to becoming the steel provider for all the warring sides regardless of nationality. They certainly had the technology. The problem was they didn't have the needed labor, so the company began to assemble a workforce in a town which half a century earlier had been a mediaeval monastery village. By the year 1912 Krupp employed over seventy thousand workers, which by the standards of the time, was amazing. The influx of large numbers of workers caused huge social, sanitary, medical, and even political problems. The Krupp Company started to build employee housing with terraced gardens, theaters, schools, libraries, etc. They actually built a new town with facilities far better than their workers had previously experienced and even introduced an elementary form of social security. The results were actually better than expected. Krupp plants were soon populated with workers so loyal, dedicated, and healthy that in the twentieth century Krupp steel almost won Germany two world wars in both of which Germany stood virtually alone against the rest of the world. The idea of planned cities spread elsewhere in Europe but in a much more limited fashion with much less success. Henry Ford did precisely the same thing in Detroit.

Among several other efforts, there is a town in Maryland called Columbia which is, by any standards, a "new town" in the sense it was deliberately built from scratch as a series of small connecting villages, each with its own community center, shopping facilities, sports areas, and so on. All the homes were located convenient to all the facilities including schools, day care centers, senior centers, and shopping. All were connected by pathways suitable for walking and bicycling. This town was originally built and financed by private capital with many problems along the way but it was intended as a modern show town where people worked, lived, and played in the same town. It is designed to fit a wide variety of budgets as well as a spectrum of occupations, where people could buy "starter" houses and work their way up to more sumptuous quarters. The plan was to deliberately include a diversity of languages, races, and cultures in order to broaden the potential owner market and so residents could experience the real world. Columbia was built with the design parameter of permanent residence, a condition with largely lost resonance these days. However, in the perspective of a technology based community which affords its citizens facilities and lifestyle, it was one of the forerunners of the future.

As is typically the case for introducing new technologies, the hurdles are not with the technology but with the politics and the economics. Much of the time the technical alternatives are near at hand but acceptance is out of reach. The Western world's energy is based almost completely on burning something. We are burning in a few centuries what took nature hundreds of millions of years to produce. In fact, the American per capita energy usage *efficiency* has improved—for instance for home lighting and heating. However, our infatuation with gas guzzling automobiles continues—at least for the moment, and our per capita *use* of energy—even aside from the automobile, continues to rise. Time was within recent memory, when you turned an electric appliance "OFF" it ceased to use energy. No longer! Electrical equipment is now specifically designed to "stay on line" regardless of the on-off condition, if only to be able to respond to remote control units. Modern security systems, answering machines, cable boxes satellite systems, radios, television receivers, VCR's, internet terminals, and cable boxes are literally always "ON" even when the consumer is elsewhere.

[20]The power industry has been deregulated which means, in theory, the consumer can choose from whom he buys power. Deregulation should encourage the growth of alternative sources such as wind power, solar power, hydro-electric power, etc.—the so-called "green power" vs. the conventional "brown power". It is intended to provide the companies with the incentive to continually increase their investment in alternative power generation. Giving people the ability to

shop for sources allows them to make "green vs. brown" selections and gives the renewable energy providers a source of revenue, for the first time. While the prices for renewable energy are not yet quite competitive with hydrocarbon fuels, they are becoming more so with time and politics. If, for instance, there is an international oil crisis, the balance between renewable energy and fossil energy would shift abruptly and dramatically in favor of green customers and interestingly, therefore in favor of local community generation sources. Local generation will make both the communities and the nation less vulnerable to threats. It avoids expensive investment in large central plants, reduce transmission losses over long lines, and allows economic choices for poor communities. This last is so evident that third world nations, the home for most of the world's population, are now actively considering such installations as their major power sources.

The total energy reaching the earth from the sun as energy every minute is more than we can ever use in a year—witness all the vegetation and animal life. (In the American northern hemisphere the sun radiates something like three thousand watt hours per day on a single square meter of surface) We have not yet learned to capture much of it in a cost effective and non-polluting manner. However, we will get there and sooner rather than later. Wind power is at this time the fastest growing source of energy. Theory suggests that power generated in three or four low population density states such as Texas could generate the electric power used by the entire continental United States. The economics of wind power are getting more attractive. From an unreliable $1.00 a kilowatt hour twenty years ago, it is down to a very reliable four cents in selected areas. If that figure drops another penny or two, it would become the cheapest power available and with no environmental impact. California now generates enough wind power to supply a major city (and that is lamentably far short of the growing power needs) least eight to ten states (and many foreign nations) are seriously considering, as well as installing, wind projects.

Photo voltaic electric power generation is common enough in cameras, calculators, control systems, and even toys. Virtually all space applications, the satellites, the space station, the planet Landers, the astronauts and many military applications—much of it depends of photo voltaics (PV) for power. This has now become a very common technology, one of which almost all of us own some application. What is driving this technology is not the Buck Rogers applications, but rather the home economics aspects and that is what will change communities. PV was once over $500 a watt and is now down below $1.00 per watt or about ten cents a kilowatt hour—only two cents above the national average. If it reaches a nickel a kilowatt hour, Edison's classical generators will have competition.

Think of the potential. Towns, corporations, institutions, and even individual homes could have their own independent power sources during daylight hours. Third world economic development is said to be more confined by the price of oil than by any other single impediment. The cost would substantially decrease and in fact, it is the third world, with little power distribution over long distances, which is anxiously supporting PV development particularly for schools, hospitals, and public facilities. Many countries, including Japan, Germany, and Italy, are not only subsidizing photo voltaic systems of varying scale, but actually installing them.

We have not even touched on a heating system which is appearing on more homes. It's called "solar heating". Already being marketed (sometimes in the wrong places) it is so simple in concept that if there is another oil crisis it's very likely to spread more rapidly than any other. Solar water heating systems simply run water through black pipes installed on roof tops. The sun heats the pipes and the pipes heat the water. Making water hot for heating homes or bathing is easily controlled by thermostatic valves and this system probably can be used economically over half the United States. The problem is more in the way of aesthetics than function. Having a roof covered with black pipes or camouflaged pipes doesn't do much for the value of the house. It still needs backup for cold or sunless days and, of course, at night. Still, there are places in the US sunny virtually all year, and aesthetics are a solvable problem. Solar heating, in fact, is almost required in countries like Israel. On the other hand, using solar energy for generating electricity is neither simple nor as cheap. This is another approach which is being worked on and the probability of solution is very still questionable. If solar energy systems begin to generate electricity economically via which ever means, the aesthetic complaint will vanish virtually overnight and such a development will change the architecture and function of towns and communities in very spectacular attributes. Roofing materials, insulation, and structural designs will need to be adjusted to accommodate additional weight and new aesthetics. Electrical sensing and switching systems will need to be installed to coordinate power and heating between the house solar supply and the conventional external energy resource (as, for instance at night or on cloudy days). For the purposes of house and water heating, modifications will be required for source selection. Town planning, zoning, and building regulations will need to be modified. Architectural practice and training will undergo major revision.

In terms of alternate energy sources, hydrogen is theoretically available. It can be "burned" to produce heat and power with no pollution at all, the residue being pure water. It's even plentiful (but not freely "available") although "hydrogen stations" would need to become as ubiquitous as gas stations. The real current problem is that hydrogen produces more pollution in sourcing than it saves in burning. Aside from manufacture and infrastructure, considering the hazards of the roads, the danger of explosion would leave few passengers willing to buy hydrogen powered automobiles and fewer insurance companies willing to underwrite them *at this point in time*. But there is one hydrogen technology which is already coming close to being viable in power stations, and potentially in homes. It's called fuel cells. In principal it should be cheap. Everyone has done high school experiments where electricity is used to separate water into its component atoms of hydrogen and oxygen. The fuel cell simply reverses the procedure to output electricity. In addition to electricity, the output is water of a very high purity. With fuel cells, there are no externalities but the cost of the system is higher and, with the economics of the moment, still uncompetitive. That too is changing. With an improving storage technology, the largest future market might be automobiles, and auto manufacturers have sunk several billion dollars into the fuel cell technology. Every threat, real or perceived, from OPEC animates this research and hastens the day of success. Interestingly, that potential helps keep oil prices down in an oil producer effort to make all the other energy resources less attractive.

[11]These technologies are being actively pursued with progress, faster is some than in others, being made in all of them. They are at the point where a breakthrough in any of them will make combination applications highly viable. Mass marketing of combinations would result in serious reductions in fossil fuel use—possibly in excess of fifteen percent. Such technologies would also tend to "localize" or decentralize energy production. They might change the economic architecture of the world.

Of course, the alternate approach uses nuclear fission or nuclear fusion, the same energy source as the sun. Fission power is already widely used as a heat source, literally in place of burning coal or oil, to generate electricity with steam turbines. Fusion is still highly theoretical. While neither produces atmospheric pollution under nominal conditions, the "waste" product of fission is so dangerous storage is becoming an international security issue. There are other facets of nuclear energy production with community implications which are important to consider from the point of view of twenty first century directions. Fission generation requires massive inputs of capital for technologies which are intrinsically dangerous in friendly hands and downright threatening in unfriendly hands. In an age of growing terrorism, that is of vital importance. Even in the best of circumstances this source of electricity further centralizes and depersonalizes this most important resource of community life in a stage whose most obvious trend is the exact reverse. Fusion, on the other hand, produces no toxic waste other than the containment vessel in which the reaction occurs—far less and much more manageable. The fuel for fission is uranium, itself a very toxic material which is not abundant, but is abundant enough for this purpose. The fuel for fusion is hydrogen, probably the must plentiful atom in the universe. Unfortunately, no practical technology has yet been developed for sustaining a fusion reaction in an economical manner and while it would be risky to predict failure of this effort, it is realistic to recognize a successful outcome is not on the horizon.

On the positive side of continued large scale central power generation there is an emerging technology which might be the "sleeper" of the situation. The technology is called "super-conductivity". Its' most simple explanation is that the normal resistance of "conductors" to the flow of electricity is significantly minimal in certain materials for which reason they are called "super-conductors". In the United States alone we use about two hundred billion barrels of oil a year, and one hundred million tons of coal, not to mention one hundred nuclear plants, thousands of hydro-electric plants, wind plants, thermal generators, tidal generators, and sundry other innovations to generate electricity. More than one quarter of all the energy produced by all of those means is lost to the resistance of the long lines used to transfer electric energy from where it is produced to where it is used. The existence of superconductors is well established but until recently the known examples of such phenomenon existed only at extremely low temperatures (4 degrees Kelvin)—an uneconomical working condition which also presents security problems. However, since their discovery, much effort and investment has begun to show progress with some super conduction occurring at the temperature of liquid nitrogen, a much more practical range. More research is continuing with the hope room temperature superconductors might even be possible. Indeed, a super conductive material (magnesium diboride) has recently been announced at thirty nine degrees Kelvin. In any event superconductivity is another one of those technologies which might transform the workplace in general and community life in specific because it will make electric generation and transmission more efficient. It makes local (as well as central) generation more practical.

[2][7]Traffic jams are probably the most immediately avoidable of energy wastes and a world wide community problem. New technology provides the most accessible world wide response. Some approaches to traffic sensing are very sophisticated, but some are amazingly simple with evident effectiveness. Japan is installing a radio system for minute to minute traffic information at all intersec-

tions which permit drivers to make intelligent choices in real time. The European Union is experimenting with the "Prometheus Program". It is a hybrid of high and low tech traffic management which, for instance controls traffic lights on a minute to minute basis depending on the relative volume of traffic in each direction of the intersection. The Prometheus System will ultimately include the "Global Positional System" on which American manufacturers are focused. The GPS is a satellite based approach which locates the car within feet of its actual position on the map and displays the position on a video map within each car. The driver enters the address of his intended end point (the GPS automatically recognizes his current position) and the system provides optimum trip driving instructions taking account, not only of start and finish locations, but of optimum individual road driving conditions as well., along with the detailed video maps. General Motors, Ford, and several Japanese and European manufacturers as well as rental agencies like Hertz, Avis, and National are already offering such accessories on selected models. One European system (the Dual Mode Route Guidance System) selects the optimum route considering distance and traffic, and informs the driver. There are other devices now in process of test such as infra-red sensors which see through fog and darkness. Still another is ultra-sonic sensors which permit automatic cruise control that apply either brake or gas appropriately. Using GPS and other sensors, self steering vehicles will become entirely practical. Digital automobiles will not only be computer controlled, they will be coupled to road conditions and to route and all such devices coming soon in recent automobile technology will conserve energy and change the economies of communities.

These all seem like "star war" fantasies but in fact are entirely practical. Most of them, in one form or another, were developed for the U.S. military and have been in use for years. A German automobile technology supplier (Bosch) expects to market this extensive type of auto control, together with engine temperature control, transmission shift control, electronic braking, and including fuel and electricity consumption control by the year 2005. (Their braking system actually produces electricity instead of heat with no brake pads involved.) The company claims the microprocessor management package will enable an internal combustion engine to achieve as much as eighty miles per gallon with very significantly reduced pollution. All commercial air traffic and a growing part of the private air traffic already make use of partial versions of this kind of automatic flight control equipment. The flight plan itself has been automated. A pilot simply keys his trip plan into the equipment which then literally "flies" the airplane almost reducing the pilots to "fall back safety equipment". Pilotless airplanes and driverless automobiles are entirely feasible but there are huge insurance implications for a litigious nation such as ours. Where is the insuring company which would take on such a risk. The technology even has political and economic implications. It isn't hard to imagine law suits based on the *lack* of such equipment built into roads and sidewalks. None the less, it is only a matter of time. Smart cars are on the way which will, by every estimate, improve driving conditions and community traffic law enforcement.

It is all very well to produce "smart cars" but the smartest car will still produce pollution. (In some cities of Japan the air is so polluted the government made "oxygen stations" publicly available.) In this regard as well, there are currently available and emerging solutions most of which are technically practical. Japanese has lowered their auto exhaust limits many times with little resulting damage to their auto industry. Bus systems, like the MARTA in Atlanta, Georgia are running on compressed natural gas (CNG). The Ford Motor Company has experimental automobiles running on CNG as well. There are also experimental cars running on combinations of gasoline, electricity, and methanol, the most interesting of which is a hybrid of gasoline and electric power. Electric power automobiles are not a new idea. At the early beginnings of the auto boom, almost half the cars on the road were electric powered. Electric cars have advantages and some real problems. High torque/low speed motors which become low torque at high speed are such an old art they are no longer considered "technology". Electric motors have the immense advantage of simplicity, i.e., easy maintenance, and very long useful life. This architecture eliminates the need for multi-speed transmissions (although top speed remains a problem). The motors become dynamic brakes during slow-downs and stops. The inherent problem of electric cars is the battery power. Batteries are heavy. A gallon of gasoline weighs under ten pounds while the batteries which could produce an equivalent amount of energy weigh several hundred pounds and replacing batteries every few years would probably produce ecological distress with environmental lead pollution. In addition batteries have limited power storage, and respond to weather conditions. The practical recharge range is something like one hundred miles. Still, calculating equivalent running costs, urban electric cars would be competitive if gas were priced at around four dollars a gallon, which is actually lower than European Union gas right now.

The hybrid gas/electric car attempts to overcome the battery limits by charging the batteries with an on-board motor/generator. The electric motor(s) help the gas motor accelerate, and in turn act as brakes when slowing. (The electric motor brakes generate usable electricity during deceleration.) Hybrids of this type somewhat achieves the best of both worlds. Mileage is dramatically up (150 miles per gallon theoretically, but now only about fifty to eighty miles per gallon actual) while pollution is dramatically down. The driving range is actually higher. A number of those models are currently on the road.

All of technology is going to result in very basic community planning revisions. American suburbia is currently designed around the oil powered automobile. (Automobile numbers are increasing at about twenty million vehicles a year world wide.) Those towns will need to be re-planned for alternate transportation as well as alternate automotive technology. Their residents will need to be convinced over time of the real advantages of transportation alternatives. They are substantial, not the least of which is public transportation. It is much more energy efficient. For illustration, the BTU per passenger kilometer of a car is around 5000. Rail and bus are less than 500 and you don't get to park the train. From a city planning point of view, a bus system in a committed lane can move an average of thirty thousand passengers an hour past a particular point, while the same lane moving private cars with four passengers will move less than eight thousand people past the same point in the same hour. And finally, from the consumer's position, he pays close to forty cents a mile in real terms to commute in his car while only paying fifteen cents average for public transportation. In an age of oil and employment insecurity, those realities may re-open the public debate on this subject.

Just as an interesting aside, the Europe Union is turning public transportation into an art. The classical design intent of any transport system is to move the people and material from one place to another rapidly and economically. The French TGV now runs at 185 miles per hour and has been recorded at three hundred. When you consider airport delays, even conventional trains show up pretty well and high tech bullet trains are spreading. The modern ambition includes easy access and minimum collateral damage. Travel has become much more convenient, and isolation more difficult. The rail system is helping the Europeans retain a most valued possession, their history. [7] Rails lines make it possible for visitors to reach ancient sites without spreading the blights of highways and pollution that contribute to the destruction of history. In the age of the automobile, the Europeans are cleaning up their traffic with trains, not roads. The metropolitan subway systems are a wonder to use. Most have rubber wheels and are amazingly silent. In many cities such as Paris and London, the subway stations are so proximate many are actually in sight of each other. (In Paris, stations are about eighteen hundred feet apart.) European Main Street technology has undoubtedly been behind the United States, but their energy policies probably will ultimately be judged more advanced.

In one contention which may, in the end, outweigh all these other considerations, urban automobile transportation is simply inefficient. Productivity, i.e., efficiency, is *the* key competitive advantage of modern technology. No matter how extensively driving is automated in terms of "smart cars", it will remain a low yield, i.e., product dollar per man-hour-dollar input to the national economy. Like the national bill for environmental maintenance, transit miles to and from work are not directly accounted for on corporate balance sheets but do become part of corporate planning in the context of labor availability. And they are, even now, part of a corporation's tax bill. As all the other labor costs shrink, that one will loom relatively larger and ultimately will become part of their calculation. Public transportation in the United States comprises only about five percent of job related travel and even that is a skewed figure. New York alone, with extensive public transport, made up more than one quarter of the total. Some current studies indicate at least 30 urban areas have or should have rail transportation, *before it is actually needed.* Those without this foresight will, in the end, lose out in the dynamics of the next century's competitive community growth.

Walking and cycling are means of transportation rarely considered although they are ancient and reliable. In a society architectured on the automobile, neither of those two options is viable but a world structured more around the microprocessor than the car will change all the rules. It is also going to change all the conventional assumptions of city planning. If more people will be working at home, fewer facilities such as gas stations and parking will be needed. Many new communities will be designed as "campus" type facilities where people live and work in the same community much as they did before the automobile overtook industry. [1] Most auto trips are five miles or less so the communities will need continuous foot and bicycle paths with expedient, safe access to shopping, eating and schools. As a parallel advantage, town planning of that kind might slow auto traffic but make walking more desirable to say nothing of healthier. Many towns already restrict cars as well as parking in city centers, shopping areas, and transit for which "bike and ride" facilities are beginning to be seen in place of "park and ride". Train passengers with bicycles will not be unusual as is the case in Europe. That opens more space for socializing and for shops. Just by way of information, the European Union's experience with such experiments indicates this practice actually generates substantial increases in the small business sales as a direct result. It is highly likely that as cities modernize, the city centers will more likely be pedestrian. The next ring is expected to be mostly pedestrian, bicycle, and mass transit. Only the outside ring will include automobiles.

Nevertheless, automobile performance will continue to improve and they will remain as a very long-term fixture on the American (and European) landscape. Cheaper and more powerful microprocessors will modify both automobiles and automobile based city planning in another subtle manner. Cars will grow to be more electronically operated as well as more dependable. Malfunctions will be pinpointed by the on-board computer and the automobile of the future will very likely follow the same "plug in" pattern as has virtually all other electronic equipment. It will produce fewer break-downs and potentially, more self service types of repairs. Service stations, as we now know them, will change both in function and in occurrence. Increasing reliability combined with greater energy efficiency and energy diversity, will reduce the need for neighborhood service stations and eventually eliminate the need for specialty service such as radiator (there won't be any), transmission repair (there won't be any), and possibly even body shops. (The current mavens forecast *owner* interchangeable bodies.) Furthermore, the lifespan of electric (and even hybrid) cars will be substantially increased. Electric motors last much longer than gas engines as is illustrated by the fact most people have the original electric motor in air conditioners in which the compressor has been serviced several times. Ditto their refrigerator. If such longevity comes to pass, the entire automotive industry will metamorphose into an entirely new industry with fewer plants, fewer sales showrooms, and fewer refuel stations. It is very hard to escape the perspective that the automobile based scene of the recent past is going to be very different in the next.

As a kind of perspective, there is one very limited vital resource with which science hasn't, and probably won't make any significant progress. The resource is water. It's hard to see water as a limited resource since for much of the West it seems as available as the nearest tap. How can a material which covers most of the world's surface be "limited"? Of course, the answer is water itself is not short, but potable water is indeed short. In fact a small fraction of one percent of the water in the world is potable. In one way or another, fresh water is used in every process known to man and in quantities much too large to consider transporting so in much of the world, water is actually more valuable than the oil we ourselves currently value so highly. (Benjamin Franklin once observed "one only knows the price of water when the well is dry".) Water is at least one contributing reason for many great conflicts of history, as for instance, the current Israeli-Palestinian war. Desalinating water is expensive. It is environmentally damaging and in any case would be limited to habitats with some proximity to oceans. Waste water treatment, commonly used in the United States to "recycle" water is not cheap—somewhere around fifty cents per cubic meter. In an attempt to use technology, the Middle-East has considering floating icebergs from the Antarctic to their ports just to melt the water for creature use.

Human water consumption has risen by over three hundred percent in the last half century. In view of the shortage of water which already exists, it is likely the people of the near future are going to undergo some forced water use revisions starting from the lawn restrictions up to consumption limits. We have spoken of gas guzzling automobiles and we should recognize most grasses are water guzzling. Populations keep growing and covenant committees continue to insist on grass ground cover. (American grass lawns cover an area about the size of the state of Kentucky even though many very attractive deep rooted plants are available which don't need all that water or attention.) There are many millions of acres of lawn, each acre of which takes as much as twenty five thousand gallons a month just to keep the grass green. Cosmetic grass is a ground cover almost unique to the United States. Grass is also an expensive cosmetic which needs constant attention—fertilizing, liming, insecticiding, and hardly least, cutting. Many of the popular grasses are non-indigenous, i.e., not local varieties, which are forced to grow in an unfriendly environment. All of these collateral considerations can be provided for a price, but water shortages affect the entire community, not merely the lawn owner.

Every water district specifically knows the extent of their water resources and for most, water availability is fixed. In spite of that knowledge, the development continues unabated. Among the many changes coming, it isn't very risky to predict water considerations such as recycling, sewage, industrial, agricultural, and particularly home use, will come under much more scrutiny. Regulations are already beginning to appear. Some states and communities are enacting land use rulings specifically regarding protection of water shed areas, as for instance the Carolinas, New England, New York, Georgia, and more every year. There may be some marginal technological improvements in the future, in the way of water saving appliances, automatic tap shut-offs, flow restrictors, computer managed usage, etc., but at least so far, this is a national problem that has not been substantially resolved by any means other than demand management. For the American community of the future, resolution will increasingly include legal water limitations and substituting drought tolerant ground cover for grass.

[12][13]Generally overlooked is the impact of technology on that ancient staple of civilization—trash. Trash turns out to be a major tool in the tool chest of archeologists because it is probably the greatest common feature of every society

in history. Indeed it is often the most permanent record of human habitat and never before has the human race accumulated trash at the rate modern homes produce it. Not for nothing is our society called the "throw-away" economy. And here too technology will have a major influence on our communities. Not only are we generating more common trash, we are generating more exotic trash. Computers, cars, television sets, refrigerators, plastics, synthetics, packaging, fertilizers, insecticides, and even explosives, not to mention the number of toxic materials so dangerous they can't be dumped in land fills—metals, radio-actives, medical materials, right down to batteries and refrigerants. Our nuclear power generation trash—spent fuel—is said to be among the most dangerous materials ever produced by man and calculated to remain dangerous for at least ten thousand years. Every community, large or small will be forced to deal with this rapid accumulation which, with any level of long term anticipation, will demand much more basic planning than was the past practice.

But if technology created the problem in the past, technology will also shape the answers in the future. Our commercial equipment is getting smaller as well as lighter. Radios which once required two people to move are now pocket sized. Computers which once blocked an entire desk will soon be included as features of cell phones. As women join the high-tech work force, more families will "eat out" routinely with the likelihood cook stoves as well as refrigerators will start downsizing, a process which not only reduces the absolute size of products, but sharply reduces the per-unit material. In other words, it expends less natural resource which in turn restrains commodity prices and environmental impact. (The forecast also dovetails with the anticipation that a migrant labor force will induce a trend toward smaller houses) On the other hand, lower costs encourage wider use. One of the computer "guru's" commented that if historical automobile productivity had kept pace with actual computer productivity growth, a Rolls Royce would be so cheap it wouldn't be worth producing.

Nevertheless, trash disposal will remain an ever growing problem for the communities of the future and will become a very large aspect of community design and personal behavior. Until recently natural resources were so abundant that those nations possessing them were among the poorest nations in the world. Even oil, with all its problems became just another commodity, while the buyers of those commodities, the industrial world, were, in contrast, the "rich' nations. The reason, of course, was that the commodity itself, disregarding all other factors such as environmental damage and ultimate disposal, was indeed cheap. In time to come, how we use commodities—and how we dispose of them—will become part of the pricing structure of the commodity. Waste disposal will become much more dynamic than mere "removal". Nuclear power was once forecast to be so cheap metering would become a waste of time. It turned out disposing of the nuclear fuel has become a major cost in the production of nuclear electricity and it is not merely the problem of the federal government. Each community will need to deal with moving such material and it is an economic as well as a security problem. If there is any doubt of this statement, one might consider asking any citizen living within a hundred miles of Three Mile Island (or a thousand miles of Chernobyl)

Mother Nature has designed a system whereby the trash of each species is used by another species or another purpose. Companies normally site plants where symbiotic industries already exist. In order to reduce the sheer volume of trash output, it will likely become wise to include waste as one of the factors influencing community negotiations for corporate location choices. Even more proactively, communities will make the effort to acquire contiguous industries where the discards of one product become the raw materials of another. Only as one possible illustration, paper plants might be enticed to locate near clothing producers since cloth remnants are often used in the manufacture of paper. Much of the farmer's actual output is wasted because most of the plant is not actually his target product, as for example the stalks. Research funding is accelerating to produce secondary products—making paper out of stalk material instead of trees. City planners will be actively looking for such symbiosis.

In the early 1980s, municipalities became aware that about ten percent of their solid waste crisis was due to a single source, polystyrene. Recognition drew so much political heat the industry formed the National Polystyrene Recycling Company (NPRC) dedicated to developing recycling applications for this ubiquitous plastic. It is used in the food industry, in the thermal insulation industry, and just about every other product because it is a packaging material. Polystyrene is virtually indestructible and for municipal landfills, indestructible trash will become a major problem.

Summary:

This current era is only decades old, and life everywhere on Earth will never be the same again. Nowhere is that state of affairs more obvious than in our neighborhoods. They once seemed to be the social center of life. Residence was pretty much permanent. Relationships were long term. Work was traditional. The structure itself seemed immutable. Lots of people knew each other by first name. The tailor, the postman, and their doctor might be Saturday night poker partners. That wasn't only "Smalltown, USA". That was New York City, USA. In the process of a single living generation, that all is vanishing.

[2][4]American technology is moving so fast the market life of some products is measured in months. That forecasts diminished term plant locations and more volatile factory jobs. It, in turn, minimizes the probability of permanent residence anywhere. Among temporary residents as well—working women, single parent families, an aging population, immigration,—their influence will combine to impel adaptation. On the other hand, current high tech communications permits a growing number of information workers to operate out of their homes without regard to the location of their corporate desk. This very unusual blend of residents will add up to serious transformations in the way communities will be constructed to indulge their citizens.

In addition, the advent of secondary energy sources along with more energy efficient automotive equipment will trim down the old oil centered economy. Community planned transportation features such as filling stations, garages, auto roads, traffic control, and toll roads will see great evolution in the next few decades. New technologies will encourage the development of small scale electric power generation. Fossil fuels will have competition from solar energy conversion. As total dependence on fossil fuels fades by substitution, by regulation, or for national security, the physical appearance of cities will begin to be adapted to a more resource efficient lifestyle. Utility infrastructure such as power lines, gas distribution, and even phone lines will experience change as the local energy sources become more available. New entertainment resources will add further impetus to modified town planning. One likely outcome will have theaters projecting newly released motion pictures from online sources rather than film cans. It will change the configuration of theaters. Included in those modifications will be new technology building codes relating to fiber optic cable installations, solar energy installations, in-house local area network distribution, central lighting, and very likely central home equipment control distribution, all of which will make buildings more energy efficient.

It sounds too dramatic to be realistic, but that is precisely the total impact of the digital technology modernization. Its consequences proliferate with astonishing velocity and remarkable impact. No nation has been able to slow it or resist it and, indeed those who tried are experiencing social upheavals in response. The United States is the creator and the big beneficiary of most of this technology so American municipalities will share in the benefits. Still, it is a very radical cultural change and there is no doubt the conversion is going to exhibit growing pains. In any case, there is no going back to "the old ways" so the best strategy for dealing with the makeover would probably be to make the conversion as quickly as possible. While this country, almost alone, is still balking at adapting the metric system, in most other aspects, we are the most adaptable nation in the world. It is unlikely any major problem with a changing world will initiate here.

The metamorphosis is going to have very significant effect on the political construct of communities. Stable areas usually develop political character based mostly on self interest. They were usually homogenous in some very primary way—wealth, ethnicity, religion, or even the majority relationship to a particular industry or plant as for instance, Detroit to the automobile industry. The old political wisdom holds "all politics are local". In an age dominated by the dichotomy between the skilled and the unskilled, as well as the settlers and the transients, local issues are very likely to experience significantly diminishing attention. For the transient segment of the population national policy will obviously assume increasing weight because those policies will impact them wherever they might go. It will be an important consideration because most won't have any idea where they will be in a few years, for that matter, next week. Even for those with the opportunity to stay put, information workers are by definition not local in lifestyle. That is not to say local issues will be unimportant, but rather they will have a different perspective. Political parties, as an illustration, are usually the mechanism to achieve some desired purpose but different places mean different parties and transients are much less likely to "join" a party if membership might be ineffective elsewhere. This possibly small shift will probably have major political consequences because national candidates are not infrequently elected by minority swings. The majority control of the senate in the year 2000 switched parties due to the affiliation change of a single senator who will go down in the history books because of his switch.

Technology has made obsolete many of the most strongly held beliefs regarding the traditional American family, the American community and the relationship of industries to both. The demographics of our population is shifting and will transform more dramatically and more rapidly than ever before. There is no longer any archetypal American nor is there any unique American family type description so the twentieth century vestiges of "hometown USA" are going the way of nineteenth century's "Life on the Mississippi". Beyond the immediately personal, an emerging pattern of "temporary" employment will significantly modify our relationship to place as well as people. Moving away from hydrocarbons as an energy source will extensively alter not only how we use energy but how much of it we can use as well. And it is not even a slight exaggeration to say that switching from an American production economy to a global information economy will produce a nation very unique in world history. All of it combined will be experienced not merely in personal terms but even more intensely in our communal constructions. Our towns will be built for greater diversity of population and purpose. They will be built to accommodate temporary populations and adapted to new technologies which change even as they are announced.

[21]And finally, America will come to recognize another type of "town" entirely new to the era. That society is the Internet community. It doesn't exist in a physical place and is usually referred to as a "virtual" community but it is very real nevertheless. Electronic villages are typically peopled by citizens who have a very unambiguous, sometimes narrow reason to be part of a specific electronic group. Because of this peculiarity, and unlike physical towns with physical real estate, network communities are often initially homogenous in at least some one aspect. The interest might be politics, music, religion, hobby, environmental, or even some socially marginal subject like race. Or, it might just be the need for "family" in a global world in which families will often be remote. Because of its uniqueness and its tight association with the growing phenomenon of Internet, it's impossible to predict where virtual associations are going in this next era, but it is safe to say they will not remain secondary. As this media matures, the network associations will develop protocols of internal social behavior, responsibilities, courtesy standards, even rituals and much of the other paraphernalia of communal living. Even the government is going to put its nose under this camel's tent.

An Internet neighborhood uses e-mail, message boards, and chat rooms rather than city halls and malls. As in any other public situation, entering a strange chat room will feel very much like being a new member in an old club. The Internet affords new members a level of protective ambiguity unique to this form of association and that makes the Internet a particularly attractive asset for rapidly changing modern communities. Local Web sites will be set up as a kind of modern "commons" by virtually every town together with public service access in libraries, post offices, police and fire stations, city hall, and even shopping centers. The local sites will enable on-line introductions to neighbors and services as well as local issues and personalities. They will very likely be established in cooperation with civic minded local businesses whose advertisements will cover the costs of the site. Such arrangements will be set up to allow new citizens, as well as established ones, to easily find places and people who might assist them. Sooner rather than later most on-line citizens will want to meet off line to develop personal, rather than wired relationships Ultimately, community Web sites will actually strengthen millennial towns because they will act as a form of introduction among the neighborhood of strangers that contemporary towns are very likely to become. Like many of the developments we speak about here, this is not a futuristic development. There are already many hundreds of such Web sites in every state and in many neighborhoods of the United States and more coming online all the time. As a matter of fact, the phenomenon is not restricted to the United States. Local Web sites are appearing in larger towns of the European Union such as Kettering in Great Britain, Amsterdam in the Netherlands, and Brussels in Belgium. This new phenomenon is here to stay and will spread out precisely as did the telephone, except this will happen much more rapidly.

All these updates of zoning, land use, construction, traffic control, and all the rest are not only mandated by technology, they are also additional inducements to companies looking for locations. It is very clear towns are going to be forced to produce enticements to retain those industries in an era in which old-fashioned loyalties have a high competitive price. The companies might not be willing to contribute to the construction of infrastructure. Still, while the global economy forces companies to find the highest yield locations those are not necessarily the cheapest sites. Acquiring the business acumen to optimize infrastructure will become a major service function of millennial town planning which means the administrative structure of towns will evolve as much as their zoning structure. While many of those concepts are not new to large metropolises, they are going to be very tall orders for the time-honored "small town" communities of the future. Both the city fathers and their planners will need to become a great deal more creative than was their past performance. That will be the biggest change of all.

This century is going to be a very personally challenging period but one with more opportunities for diversified people than any social construct in history. This period will have too many individual and public adjustments to leave solely in the hands of impersonal expertise—corporate or government—and that will modify the politics of the next era as well. It won't always be ideal but conversion is already upon us and it will become very evident in the very near term.

Reading and Reference:

[1] Wordwatch Paper 98 Lowe

[2] *Urban and Metropolitan Economics* John M. Levy 0 07 037455 1

[3] *Probable Tomorrows* Cetron & Davies 0 312 15429 1

[4] *The Third Wave* Alvin Toffler 0 553 24698 4

[5] *Urban Neighborhoods, Networks, and Families* P.Wireman 0 669 14503 9

[6] The *Seduction of Place: the City in the Twenty-first Cent*ury J.Rykwert 0 375 40048 6

[7] *Urban Rail in America* B.Pushkarev 0 253 17965 3

[8] Networks for Homes *IEEE SpectrumMagazine*, Dec.1999 Amitava Dutta-Roy

[9] *Technology Review* Magazine, Energy Special Issue February, 2002

[10] *IEEE Spectrum* Technology Issue January 2000

[11] *Time Magazine* Special Issue June 00

[12] *Why Do We Recycle?* Frank Ackerman 1 55963 505 3

[13] *Packaging for the Environment* Stilwell, Canty, Kopf, Montrone 0 8144 5074 1

[14] "*e-topia*" W.J.Mitchell 0 262 63205 5

[15] USA Today, June 12, 2002 "Technology"

[16] *Last Oasis* Sandra Postel0 393 03428-3

[17] *Time Magazine* Special Issue November 8, 1999

[18] *The Essential Guide to Digital Set-top Boxes & Interactive TV* G.O'Driscoll 0 13 017360 6

[19] *Technology Review* Sept.2002 P22

[20] *IEEE Spectrum* April 2002

[21] *Community Building On The Web* Amy Jo Kim 0 201 87484 9

[22] *Nation Magazine* 6/21/99 Andrew Shapiro

[23] *IEEE Spectrum* September 2002 P70

[24] *Probable Tomorrows* Cetron & Davies 0 312 15429 1

4

Politics: Changing Perspectives

The range of available personal decisions open to most American citizens of this era is simply unprecedented. Occupations will be untraditional. Residence will be transitory. Marriage will be nominal. Religion will be optional. Economic class will be more fluid. Even nationality will be more ambivalent. All of those options will be substantially influenced by personal judgment. For the political process, the Internet has opened a Pandora's Box of mixed possibilities, the extent of which cannot even be fathomed as yet. [11]The electronic networks will all provide the predominant outreach basis of political behavior, much as did radio singularly provide it during the '30s and television since then. This time, though, the body politic will be able to "talk back".

The most enthusiastic proponents of Internet politics see the e-nets as restoring the original Greek forums unencumbered by politicians. The autocrats around the world, they claim, will lose control of their populations. Proponents of our representative form of government have forecast the enormous access to information will even make political parties obsolete thus eliminating the need for compromise. Much has been made of the implied corruption of a money soaked political contributions party system. [3]With the Internet at the end of your kitchen table, it is hard to argue that the corruption of contributions would be moderated by an inexpensive, direct connection between voter and candidate. Indeed, some fear all major issues might be decided by instant polls, usually at the expense of thoughtful consideration and expertise. It is called "direct democracy. It might actually happen, but the reality as of this point is not yet evident in spite of the explosive spread of the e-net.

In most of history, the course of events was determined by the affluent and the influential—usually one and the same people. In the next century, information, an ancient ruling monopoly, will become an available resource to anyone looking to break that dominion. Extensive public access to information will not only impinge on who is held responsible for our political destinies, it will radically modify how we will select them as well as what we expect of them. Increasingly widespread e-nets will permit every citizen the opportunity to have an opinion about alternatives as well as the opportunity to express those attitudes to the top of the political ant hill. It is going to make propaganda and hypocrisy a bit more difficult. Freedom derives from demand, but power from exercise and exercise will become more convenient. Challenges to the habitual will be resisted even by many of its beneficiaries but mounting public engagement will at least be an escalating individual pick in this environment of rising public detachment. The down side will be a net loss of the ancient sanction for lethargy called "trust". The down side is those who choose to be spectators despite any convenience of engagement. They will easily find cronies with whom to commiserate. I suppose it should be comfortable to know some things never change.

The modern Luddites (workers who, in the early nineteenth century, objected to the introduction of machines in factories) in our midst pine to return to the good old days before the Internet. Electronic politics, they feel, is removing the human content, the "demos" from "democracy". Only fifty years ago, the same apocalypse forecasters thought television would take the debating out of *elections*. The doomsday protagonists insist the new Internet media is "dumbing down" America. Electronic networks will disseminate more information into more homes about more candidates than all the palm pressing and baby kissing of the "pre-e-net" era. It is just as likely people will get more involved because information will be available independent of time, and place, and even of language. In an era of impermanence, politicians will be less vested. In the long run, politics will become more accessible and the process possibly more reactive. Making "dumb" choices will at least be a matter of choice because choice is what the flood of electronic information makes possible.

Regardless of ultimate outcome, their modern Luddites have already lost the battle against the machines. [4]Access to the Internet is on the way to becoming an entitlement. More useful than TV or newspapers, the net will become a key mechanism of group action and interaction as well as global information because it cancels time and language considerations. Developing capability like voice recognition may one day permit voice reduction to approximate print and automatic translation to any language of choice. For the ethnically diverse streets of tomorrow's towns, such potential will be too politically "hot" for any politician to touch. This genie won't return to the bottle and the most foreseeable strategy for dealing with its potential political pratfalls is to shepherd its evolution around them. Political Web sites, a multitude of which now exist, can navigate interested citizens through issues and steer them toward local political action meetings.

Web pages will be used by active citizens to communicate directly with any level of government and any office holder. Opinion surveys will be instantaneous, secure, and eventually even scientific. The Web pages will also be used by citizens to communicate with each other, at their own convenience and out of their own homes—or wherever the Internet stations are set up. They won't just be voyeurs of the process, they will be active participants. The old adage "If you don't vote, you can't complain" will revert to "If you're not part of the action you're part of the problem".

Politics has always been bounded by place but many issues which were locally centered are becoming global, such as the Kashmir conflict or Chechnya terrorism. A very short time ago, very few could identify those areas. In America, the colonial conflict between local and non-local powers is almost as vociferous as they were in the eighteenth century. But many issues are being recognized as clearly non-local. [10]Women's interests, if not really universal, are certainly among the most obvious borderless concerns. Even in prior times, women were beginning to redefine their political personalities because of a growing awareness that the restrictions on their lives were possibly the commandments of men of this world, not the God of another. Were that not true, Saudi Arabia would have had no need for "gender police".

One always hears the old political saw "think globally but act locally". In the twenty-first century "local" is going to be a highly qualified adjective and it will blur the margins of confined ritual, including the circumstances of women or the right to tax. Everything people know about politics is directly a consequence of discourse with the world. Herr Hitler's first line of assault was one of radio propaganda. Television has changed political history. However, unlike radio and television, twenty-first century contact technology is not one way. It is difficult to exaggerate the importance of an interactive media. As a single example, with one giant leap, interactivity will encourage many more women—half the world's opinion—to become much more politically functional because it will be so easy for them to fit activity into their lives without disruption. Their participation alone will not only change the mechanics of political activity, it will change the substance.

The evolution of women's political involvement in virtually every Western nation grew apace with the ease of communications. In the last part of the last century, the acceleration of gender equality is reflective of the flood of new transmission media. In the future, women will assume active and even commanding positions in the major parties. Women in elective positions will become so commonplace as to escape novelty. The development will be enhanced not only by the growth of women's increased confidence but by the very nature of the upcoming decades. Job mobility will erode traditional political structures leaving openings for newcomers—an irresistible opportunity for women. The Internet will enable many single issue partisans to assemble electronically, another ideal opening for women who will both create and lead those groups. Corporate jobs demanding training skills will begin to favor women because they are starting to outnumber men in post high school enrollment and the same corporate experience will further encourage women's political leadership. It was once said "the hand that rocks the cradle rocks the world". I think it may be arguable but I doubt anyone will deny that in politics, the hand that distributes the donations will dominate the decisions.

It's not without reason campaign donations are now an issue. The up and coming financial force of the times are the growing throng of professional women, most of whom know who they are, and will know what they want. As their power positions improve, the women will undoubtedly differentiate among themselves with regards to money and status, much as the men have, so the "monolithic feminism" of the twentieth century will fragment in the twenty-first. The point remains, however, the women of this next century are going to be politically heard both individually and collectively as never before in any society and high technology modern communications like the Internet, the cell phone, the hand helds, etc., are going to play a considerable role in the evolution. Indeed, some nations fear the mounting political role of women is akin to revolution and that with good cause.

And not just the women. [11]The Internet, et al, will produce a new generation of voters with literally world wide discourse and global responsiveness. The networks will also become the means, probably equaling or exceeding television, to reach and influence people anywhere as well as their connections everywhere. A global advent of electronic networks will become one of those empowering events which, like the invention of the printing press, will change the way twenty-first century history unfolds. Minorities, immigrants, spin-off religions, will not only be able to link up, they will all be able to engage political entities without intermediaries. The Association for Progressive Communications (APC) was created with the purpose of promoting information access to NGOs, and PACs regarding environmental campaigns, women's rights, human rights, civil rights, and even personal crusades. Only about a single decade old, they are, by now, a consortium of over 25 member organizations which provide links to over 50,000 non-member organizations in over 100 countries. APC provides extensive support for their various movements by way of a world wide network accessible from almost anywhere and they are only a single example of how technology is changing the character of the political world.

In the United States in particular, the digital networks of the next century are going to so dominate the political scene as to determine the outcome of elections and policy debates. Even the drawback of "cost" is rapidly becoming mute as the prices of connectivity equipment of every description tumbles to the point that reading the news on line will be cheaper and far more comprehensive than buying the newspaper. In fact, as is generally true of the digital world, the cost of any kind of equipment is getting so low the profits will be generated in the connectivity service with the equipment likely to become subscription gifts—again the over-riding characteristic of the service dominated economy. As an additional supplement to considerations of cost, equipment operation is becoming so simple even keyboards will be obsolete. Voice operated equipment ("Voice Recognition"), is already appearing on research calendars. Commercial Microprocessors currently available recognize thousands of words and, of course as is generally the case, the next generation will include several orders of magnitudes greater capacity. (Hand held electronic translators for traveling in foreign lands are commonplace even now.) On Taiwan, the Philips Speech Processing Office has produced a voice recognition accessory, designed to work with standard American computers, whose most recent model recognizes tens of thousands of Mandarin spoken words. In anticipation several firms are forecasting processors which will hear in one language and output in another. One will be able to generate an e-mail in English and have it received in French, German, Spanish, and eventually even Russian and Japanese with very little training. When (not if) all this projection becomes operative, the last restraints on political activity from any part of Main Street, USA (or Shanghai Street, China) will have disappeared because many gender and cultural limitations will have vanished.

Easily available electronic networks will not necessarily promote broad consensus. More likely it will advance the proliferation of narrow interest political action groups of people who can easily find each other for the support of particular issues. The same group membership might very well be in mutual opposition in other groups and on other issues. The most difficult imperative of a very restive twenty first century will be broad accord among so many diverse, detached, and individualized smaller groups. Legitimacy will demand people be convinced their attitudes do indeed count and will be considered. In such a context, election clarity of both process and results will become a electorate priority for both parties.

The election of year 2000 graphically demonstrates both failures. Polls, in fact, suggest a large majority of Americans feel voting is a nationwide problem and supported updating election machines to ensure flexibility as well as accuracy. The first and probably most pernicious problem which will need to be dealt with is the low voter turnout—almost always less than fifty percent which means less than twenty five percent of the vote eligible citizenry determine policy for the most powerful nation in the world, which is almost tantamount to saying the miniscule minority very nearly determines the course of history. The next level of problems is the variety of voting systems. Some are lever systems. Others use punch-cards. There are actually a number of computer voting systems of various kinds. The third problem turned out to be the tally of ballots. [15]Some need to be scanned in order to be counted. In many precincts, the ballots are actually hand read. Others are entered automatically on leaving the election booth. A few systems permit the voter to correct his vote. Others are irrevocable. Not a few systems physically permit voting for excess numbers of candidates but then disqualify the ballot. Some fully qualified citizens skip voting because they have language problems and the ballot instructions are not clear or inappropriately arranged. And hardly least, many claimed they had been physically prevented from voting. Some are unable to reach the polling place within the allotted hours through no fault of theirs. And finally, not a few people are unable to operate (or reach) the voting machines due to physical inabilities.

Research teams at M.I.T. and Caltech issued a report in July of 2001 authored by a team of engineers and social scientists, claiming that well over one million actually cast votes (between two and three percent of the total) were lost or not counted due to faulty equipment. In political times such as these, where elections are decided by several thousand votes, such a level of vote loss invalidates the process. The research suggested equipment known to have faults, some of which is electronic, should be replaced by more modern electronic, preferably digital, machines. In spite of its total novelty in the field, the data indicates digital voting equipment is already at least as reliable as current standard machines.

While no system will ever satisfy everyone, a broad consensus is developing for standards for updated voting machines of the millennium. Generally, from a voter point of view, these criteria are:

1. They need to be easy to understand, access, and use, even for disabled people.
2. They need to be reliable and secure.
3. They need to be programmable in several languages.

From an operational point of view, the criteria gets more complicated. At a very minimum:

1. They need to be cost effective to buy and install.

2. They need to be tamper-proof.

3. The machine needs to positively identify both authorized operator and voter authenticity and yet maintain voter anonymity.

4. The system and the software must be easily available for authorized testing without revealing any count information.

5. The system must have audit capability which positively demonstrates the total count.

6. The equipment must be economical to maintain.

Many of those requirements might apply equally to a telephone system and telephones are everywhere. Purchase should be pretty straight forward but the only area of broad agreement is that "something needs to be done". The constraint, aside from political considerations, is the serious impediments to widespread computer voting systems. One of the most damaging is voter anxiety about his vote being counted without a paper trail. Perhaps a more long term menace is deliberate or accidental program bugs, particularly those which might not be detectable by standard tests. Even if they are all eliminated, there is always an ongoing fear of program penetration, as has happened with Pentagon online programs. Furthermore, guaranteeing voter anonymity conflicts with guaranteeing audits. It is arguable that programmed redundancy, i.e., having the vote simultaneously tabulated in several different programs, might eliminate many of those problems, and well it might. Such a plan would analytically compare the various counts and ring a failure alarm in the event of disparity, but adding programming adds complexity, failure modes, acquisition, and maintenance costs, and worst of all, it augments tampering potential.

Perhaps the greatest potential disadvantage of computerized voting outweighs all of the above. [15]The demand for easy access suggests using the Internet. Older people are more suspicious of the Internet security than are young people. (It is worth noting that business and banking use the network extensively with notably increasing numbers of elderly people subscribing to the service In spite of those hesitations, I think it can be predicted that the growth of the Internet in personal and business service situations is such that this problem of perception will very soon be dispelled.)

The experts are not all pessimistic. One interesting suggestion is to ultimately make the ballot an electronic memory card with precinct identification which is inserted into the voting booth computer. The computer displays all the positions and candidates (as well as the actual votes) and it permits corrections. When satis-fied, the voter then presses the "vote" button at which time his votes are actually printed to the card memory and "locked" for count or transfer to a counting machine. The card cannot be modified and records every "read". It is filed for audit purposes in order to guard against fraud or machine failure. Another related variation of this proposal might realize its greatest advantage after "smart ID" cards become available with difficult to forge identification such as finger or eye prints. The idea is to make voting software available through the Internet or pub-lic access—i.e., libraries, city halls, supermarkets, etc., together with sequenced voter numbers (i.e., not I.D.'s). The software permits the voters to make their choices together with corrections at their own leisure and then save them to a "floppy disc" after which the floppy is then irreversibly unalterably "locked". The disc is then "downloaded" at the polling place after proper voter identification (or using his smart ID card.) Even used in this manner, the voting process is speeded up because all the selections are pre-recorded. However, the near term hope of this variation is that with time equipment will become accessorized to PCs which will read the smart ID card. for other purposes (such as debit card) but can then be used as well to confirm voter identification so the citizen can cast his ballot by downloading the floppy over the Internet.

Another system which, is newly universal to all of Georgia is produced by Die-bold,—interestingly, the ATM company. In this approach, the voter will get a "key card" when he signs in. He inserts the card into the voting machine to access the ballot. His selections are made on a touch screen and processes through the entire "ballot" by touching the "next" screen button. When he is finished with the entire ballot, he reviews all his choices and touches the onscreen "return" but-ton to go back to any choice for correction. He can repeat this procedure until he is satisfied with all of his choices, after which he presses the "cast Ballot" screen button. The votes are stored within the machine and on a backup for both cross check and safety. After the polls close, the votes are automatically tabulated for each machine, and also transmitted to "headquarters" by modem. Diebold has included an audio channel for blind voters and/or citizens with reading or lan-guage problems. This too sounds futuristic but these devices were worked state-wide in Georgia for the 2002 election with remarkably few complaints or prob-lems.

The average American who spends too little time with his children, can hardly be expected to devote a great deal of time to political issues. As a result of this record, particularly after the Florida fiasco of election 2000, more than a dozen states proposed legislation to research at home (i.e., on-line) voting. None passed but a division of the Department of Defense has held an on-line election test involving a few thousand people and Arizona's Democratic Party ran a primary election online in the year 2000. Obviously it can be done, but there are legal and political problems involved as well as problems of security and privacy. On-line voting is on the way but probably as much as a decade away. (Keep in mind the incredible billions of dollars moving on-line every day routinely, a practice which only one decade ago was also predicted to take many more decades to happen.) Highly classified government communications move on the network every minute. I would suggest the more practical problems are likely to turn out to be homes which don't have computers or e-mail terminals, and interrupted voting connections, both of which are obviously solvable. As communities set up public access terminals in fire stations, police stations, city halls, malls, etc., the "availability" problem would disappear. As an extension, computer voting will have some fringe benefits, not the least of which will be the augmentation of on line registration. Just as a point of information, voter "registration" is almost peculiar to American elections but voter participation is higher in Europe. Registering on line at least makes the process more convenient.

Reduced cost of campaigns will probably be another benefit of the association of voting and Internet. Campaign funding has become so enormous the rich or those associated with the rich have a popularly perceived advantage which has engendered demands for legal limits on contributions to federal election campaigns. Legal limits on campaign contributions may have questionable constitutionality, but the absence of such limits yields questionable elections. The Internet is a more economical and probably more cost efficient channel to the voter base. Legal and popular acceptance of a relationship between cyberspace and the voting process will legitimatize the computer network as competition for broadcast networks which currently absorb most of the moneys spent on campaigns. Interestingly, Internet electioneering also makes response to funding appeals much easier, and even instantaneous via both Chat Rooms and e-mail thus helping the candidate measure the effectiveness of his appeals, to say nothing of his candidacy. Most important, it permits the voter to be an active participant of the democratic process. This will become very important when technology induced job relocation will tend to nullify the political "redistricting" which, for practical purposes and often by agreement of both parties, is designed to guarantee the "pre-election" of party candidates. Voter relocation will make such "arrangements" more difficult to honor. And, indeed, digital voting will make absentee voting more convenient further eroding "pre-election".

The most basic problem is that maintaining voter privacy and providing trace-able audits which, from a computer point of view, are almost mutually contradic-tory conditions. Such a check system requires an independent count mechanism from the ballot to the tabulation without individually identifying the voter him-self. In an automatic teller system the check and balance is the piece of paper the client retains and the personal audit he can challenge. No such test can exist for AVM's (Automatic Voting Machines) and without it all the voting errors of mechanical voting machines would still leave doubts for the computerized ver-sions. Undetected program errors can unintentionally add to the dilemma because the equipment test procedures would most likely not be checking for those errors. As a result, even post election test runs by auditors would not reveal their presence. Anyone who has ever bought new software can testify to "glitches" the program vendor hadn't caught. Internet voting would conceivably be even more hazardous because of the possibilities for disruption, and viruses in addition to all the above difficulties at the point of receipt.

With perfect programming, the voting equipment itself can not have guaran-teed vote precision. For example, touch screens can introduce errors by "smear-ing" an entry. Keyboards might be too expensive and too complicated an alternative for general public polling places. The screen presentation would need to be reduced to the lowest required educational level. Direct Electronic Record-ing machines (DREs) are expensive, (probably about five thousand dollars by the time they are through with all the new features) and have maintenance costs. They would probably need to be plug-in designed for quick and easy repair as well as featuring fault indicators. Card readers have serious wear problems and are more expensive than scanners (although non-rubbing card readers are already being designed). One of the constitutional problems not yet in court is the prac-tical reality that those with computer access would have voting "access" not avail-able to those without them. It is an issue implied by the campaign finance laws and it might be a fair challenge because people without modern facilities tend to be older, less educated, and far less affluent. A complaint more difficult to deal with is the "smart I.D card". The technology is now available but longstanding opposition to any NATIONAL ID cards makes their issue unlikely in the near future. "Smart" ID cards almost produce paranoid fits. However, re-issuing new (magnetic) Social Security cards, programmed with tamper proof coding, finger or eye prints, and permanent proof of citizenship, might be less objectionable and less difficult to promote. New PC's are soon going to start appearing in the mar-ket place with built in magnetic card readers which might be used to read the magnetic strip Social Security card, and that might be less worrisome for those who are concerned about national ID's. Conceivably the cards might end up being used for home voting as well as more prosaic applications.

[15]Digital voting difficulties are compounded by one additional complication. Whereas standard voting machines must be individually tampered with, or they must individually break down, in order to effectively destroy an election process. With computerized voting, the interference could occur at a single location and produce the exact same result on a widespread basis. Still, as advances in computer security and reliability are realized, it will take little more technology (as a personal option) to convert a magnetic memory card reader accessory into a reliable home based or public access voting machine. The card might later be inserted in a public card reader much like an ATM, which reads and keeps the card. The technology might also be used for opinion surveys and commercial product polls. (In fact, it might be one way to partially fund the new system). It would be as reliable as an ATM and as secure as a bank transaction.

A home based PC system would permit the actual voting to take place at any personally convenient time and hopefully increase participation. It might also be the best enticement for rural and low income citizens into the voting public. A recent congressional study determined that undercounting minority and low income ballots is not unique to Florida. The study found nationwide, poor people are three times more likely to have their votes discarded. The same study found districts with better voting technology showed markedly less disparity between groups. As a matter of interest, a proven computer based voting system appropriately simplified and illustrated might eventually be incorporated into an internationally recognized software standard supplied by the United Nations. It could then be installed and the election remotely monitored during questionable elections in places where "nation building" is occurring. (While most Americans (90% by one survey) support such a uniform national voting system, there is still no demonstrable majority supporting international computer based voting systems.)

Speaking of local news, the Internet in politics becomes another exposure for the candidates and one which is interactive. Engaging the audience is usually judged to be the best way of keeping their interest. (Example—Governor Dean in the 2004 nominating campaign) Candidates spend a great deal of their time and their resources trying to get on the TV screens, but their appearance is determined by station managers. The print media is not time constrained but is usually vulnerable to reporter's "interpretation" in the same article. On the other hand, their presence on the Internet is determined by their own selection as regards content, duration, and longevity—and it costs far less—a campaign manager's dream.

Although the "dumbing down" effect is not as widespread as feared, the era of digital networks has had one very notable outcome, already described, linked to that source. The Internet enables people with any bent of mind to easily find each other. As far back as 1985, the Anti-Defamation League published a commentary which forecast the rise of networked hate groups. The forecast turned out to be prophetically accurate with hate group web sites springing up targeting civil and abortion rights groups, minorities, gays, other religions, and even government workers—all on the Internet. Some of those group sites actually publish instructions for dangerous activities. The more sophisticated hate mongers don't describe a course of action against their "enemies" for fear of legal retaliation. Instead they often merely publish an "enemies list" which includes pictures and addresses. They inaccurately identify themselves and can present themselves on their Web pages in more positive poses than their actual persona would permit in real life. To the extent they don't specifically incite to violence, they usually calibrate their activities to fall into the first amendment realm of "free speech". The Internet is an international phenomenon and there are international laws restricting "hate speech" including Article 4 of the "International Convention on the Elimination of All Forms of Racial Discrimination" which the United States has signed and ratified. There are also laws on the books restricting e-mail threats. Some, like the European Union, with an understandable reaction to bigotry deriving from its long, horrific continental experience with the human price tag, lean toward censorship. The United States, with its traditional aversion to governmental prescriptions, leans toward public exposure of bigots. It is at least possible the technology advances will permit the "filtering" of hate messages so parents, for instance, can protect their families from exposure to this unintended outcome of the information age. With its constantly expanding access to and use of international electronic networks, the whole world is going to have to resolve the dichotomy of approach and in developing a response will have simultaneously dealt with other unwanted Internet "information" such as pornography.

Going on line is both cheaper and more efficient for the outrageous fringe. Web pages will easily include sound and motion pictures, both of which will be an additional enticement to marginalized people, often with substandard economic or educational aptitude. There are many formal groups which fall into this category such as the KKK, the National Alliance, the White Aryan Resistance, the Republic of Texas, and new gender liberated groups like Women for Aryan Unity, and Her Race. While groups like these are the larger ones, they are public and can be publicly identified. There are many others, smaller, and more anonymous, which are much more difficult to recognize. All of them, large and small are going online. This is clearly going to be the strategy of choice for extremists in the enlightened Information Age.

In America, the search for technologies to limit unwanted access is outgrowing its origins as a cottage industry to become a very major demand for restricting legislation as well as service. In totalitarian societies, those very same technologies are evolving into the tools which restrict privacy. And so, the defining political feature of Internet is not technology. It is more likely to be sociology and that salient fact will further drive widening economic performance gaps between Information and Pre-Information societies. Those who prefer the "old time religion" regardless of flavor, might soon, in this age of choice, be left with no other choice.

Summary:

J. Q. Public is going to have the absolute power to sound off out loud and clear to an audience as large as "J.Q." can attract. He will be able to instantly address the community leaders as easily as he reaches the rest of the population. He won't even need to leave home to do it and, more remarkable, leaders won't need to attend forums to listen. Politicians will be able to be engaged without the filtration of political managers or of editor's "interpretation" if they choose to be honest. But politics is a profession where some feel honesty is the worst policy so unfiltered responses might become a kind of integrity test and Internet Chat Rooms a litmus test.

This has been a time of spreading political disenchantment, well demonstrated by the dismal turnouts at the election booth. Thomas Patterson's book *The Vanishing Voter* documents the extent to which voters are oblivious of both issues and candidates. His book, sponsored by Pew Charitable Trusts gauges voter attention based on more than 80,000 interviews about the 2000 election and, no surprise, it turns out, after spending hundreds of millions of campaign dollars, both sides had managed to excite avid voter interest in scandals but only indifference to issues. Patterson attributes the apathy to many causes, among which are declining party cohesion, over-long campaigns, negative campaign emphasis, and complicated registration procedures. Technology actually will be a factor in party splintering along single issue fault lines, but it potentially enhances voter participation by making the process more convenient and simpler. By reducing language and distance hurdles, new high tech machines at the polls and in the home will at least minimize the mechanics of the political process while permitting people of like "issue" mind to organize subject based political action. It sounds like American politics might become Balkanized but the basic requirement of any democratic republic is participation and greater participation will always result in greater political diversity. In any case, third party history in America is not such as to encourage fear. In combination with the higher educational demands of this new time, that should concurrently result in greater political sophistication and more positive campaigns.

With all such assistance, one would assume this upcoming age should promote the parallel demand for at least better than average competence of our political leadership. Faulty leadership will be manifestly the public fault. Using web sites to assemble shared complaint associations provides a political means quite unique and already becoming exploited. With all the other devices available and becoming available—e-mail, scanners, wireless and pocket equipment, call answering and generating paraphernalia, all will give even small groups an outreach far beyond their group's dimensions or boundaries, further diminishing the excuse of "them" and "us". Like the churches, political parties will need to reorganize their operations to acknowledge their own diffused power and the enlarged power of smaller groups. They will be forced to recognize the urgency of the "umbrella" principal of divergence within their ranks introduced by the issue disunity of factions that were traditionally monolithic. They will be forced to accept outreach to unorthodox communities with newly growing distinctiveness.

However wider communications among more expressive diverse groups will not expand an operating American democratic system unless all that communication culminates in the ultimate American poll called an election. For this purpose it is hard to believe a world completely dominated by digital electronics is going to continue elections dominated by voting equipment designed in large part in the nineteenth century. Computerized voting and voting online does indeed have several serious challenges but, at the same time, offers economies and advantages which many feel prevail over the disadvantages so significantly it would seem impossible to refuse the challenge. And as a matter of fact, we would not even be first in this effort. Internet voting is spreading in the European Union. Great Britain has conducted a significant number of pilot Internet voting efforts. Switzerland and Italy are embarked on similar programs. (Italy expects to use "Smart Card" voter identification in combination with a personal password as voter qualification.) These European trials have been restricted to inconsequential elections because they are intended as test runs but Internet voting is very important for European politics because the E.U. has become a migrant polyglot of nationalities and languages. Internet voting will permit Union citizens to vote in their own regional elections regardless of where in the Union they happen to reside. Some experts remain skeptical of large scale (national) digital elections and the truth is there is yet to be a real test. In the United States, until very recently, online voting experiments had been more or less restricted to the Armed Services which is almost traditionally a technology leader for the nation, but this constraint is going to change almost immediately. Georgia is already equipped with touch screen polling place voting machines. If year 2002 polling place election success in Georgia is repeated in only a few other states, the momentum toward Internet voting will become overwhelming. At this point, the velocity is obviously in only one direction and the impetus is building.

The political scene of America is always changing but the entire landscape of the twenty-first century is going to be painted by technology.

Reading and Reference:

[1] *Nation Magazine* 06/21/99 Andrew L. Shapiro INTERNET-SOCIAL ASPECTS

[2] Community College Week 12/28/98 Jordan Kessler

[3] www.bostonvote.org/soundoff/voting_machines.html

[4] www.fcw.com/civic/articles/2001/0402/web-itaa-04-02-01.asp   {subjects:, internet voting, gender voting, minority voting, }

[5] the *Chronicle of Higher Education*, Aug. 3, 2001

[6] *Population Today*, Washington, August/September 2001 anonymous

[7] the *Chronicle of Higher Education* Washington; April 20, 2001 Olsen

[8] Atlanta Journal Constitution 5/4/02 Standford

[9] Atlanta Journal Constitution 9/20/01 Stanford

[10] *Women @internet* Harcourt 1 85649 572 8

[11] *Cybercitizen* Christopher Kush 0 312 26305 8

[12] *The Vanishing Voter* T.E.Patterson

[13] *Humanist Magazine* Nov.1999 Global Stat us Report 1.1.2050

[14] *IEEE Spectrum* October 2002 P46 Rebecca Mercuri

[15] *Computer Related Risks* P.G.Neumann 0 201 55805 X

[16] *Technology Review* Nov. 2002 P26

[17] *Newsweek* Magazine January 1, 2000

5

Education—The Democratic Autocracy

Within current memory, school was intended for children. The curriculum was programmed to prepare students for employment. The class schedule was predicated on a student body whose concerns centered on socialization and learning (in that order). The teaching profession was perhaps more disputed than any other because until recently it involved our children, the only aspect of our lives which has remained constant, if not stable. Researchers have described the traditional system as operating to the advantage of the affluent. Statistically the children of prosperous families started school earlier and remained in school longer so they absorbed more of the educational resources. [7]As the education of disadvantaged children improved, that of the wealthy advanced as well. In fact, as the level of the lowest economic classes improved, the value of incremented education actually decreased, so the gap in achievement changed comparatively little over the years. It sounds self contradictory, but in fact, it actually does make sense in terms of market supply and demand. As more youngsters' graduate high school, the supply of that level of education increases so the market value decreased.

School systems of the future will be dominantly attended by tax paying, voting adults, not children. For mature student bodies, remaining employable will be their incentive. Skill updates while working will be their mandate. Changing the clientele will profoundly alter the road rules of conventional education. Given the requirements of an information economy, adult working citizens will demand access to more equal education including pre-school facilities. A more diverse, voting, and likely non-Caucasian student body will inexorably demand ongoing re-training throughout the day, and very likely throughout the year. The cost of training will necessarily be shared by government, industry, and, unlike conventional public education, by the "students" themselves. Such a development will have many consequences. If industry and students are contributing to the cost of their education programs, the programs will be tailored to the desires of the sponsors, not necessarily the presumptions of the local school board. This means schedules convenient to industry and to the students. It means syllabus appropriate to their needs. It means locations expedient to their jobs. And that means teachers will be subjected to the same results oriented quality control standards for teaching performance as the students are for their learning performance. It also implies the educational syllabus will need to anticipate work which ***doesn't even exist at the time of learning***. It implies the new educational requirements will include "job adaptability"—i.e., the ability to use what you already know as a basis of learning what you need to know. It mandates the *practice* of learning. In fact, as industry necessarily assumes more responsibility for the training of the American work force, the teachers themselves will become part of the transitory work force. They will be hired by the industries either as permanent personnel or perhaps as consultants paid by the class hour much as industry now pays other employees. This circumstance implies industry might well become a major employer of teaching professionals as well as a dominating determinant of syllabus. It also implies adult students. For two income families job mobility has financial implications for professions which were previously secure.

[7] There have been an almost endless series of studies relating level of education with parental income. In fact, studies have shown that even equalizing educational attainments still leaves the students from wealthier backgrounds generally doing better than those from the lower classes. For those reasons, the widening gap between the wealthiest and the poorest Americans has great consequence in the context of education. It means less able students of higher economic origins will achieve higher education, and by implication, greater success, than more able students of lower economic class. That might be called affirmative action. In the aggressive circumstance of a technology economy this is being recognized as a very serious competitive risk for the entire nation. While there might be no practical way to actually equalize education under those circumstances, it will be minimally demanded by a growing diversity of students and subject matter that access be improved. The challenge will acquire the most fervent political impetus during the next decade. In the information age fallout, natural ability will become more commanding than ever before, which in turn means by implication, economic class margins will very likely become more porous. This outcome will not be a response to any claim to social justice, but rather to a global market demand for skills.

An additional, and complicating, customer base for this ongoing education is the rapidly growing non-English speaking immigrant community. For many American born students, continuing training is a means of advancing their life-styles. For the immigrant group, education is an implacable survival prerequisite and it is more than just likely immigrant and adult minority people will gradually make up the majority of grade school and post grade school populations. The clear implication is any training system will need to accommodate instruction needs such as foreign languages, foreign cultures, and far more sophisticated teaching technology than is currently common in most schools. They will almost certainly include more learning time outside of formal school hours. Interactive cable television will grow in importance in the teaching technology by reason of client convenience and availability. [3][4]With the advent of digital TV, the day is arriving when computer equivalent equipment will be common in American homes of every economic class. Internet schools, CD/ROM's, DVD's, and VCR tape training will all be part of the picture. Indeed, education will probably become more activity dominated and less location related. It is not necessarily an optimum outcome but it will very likely come to pass brick and mortar school facilities, like brick and mortar bank facilities, will actually devolve into a less towering status in the American educational scene. As far ranging as all of this seems, it is equally expansive for the industries themselves. The demand for unending training will prompt unions to press for reduced working hours or to incorporate training hours into working hours.

The sweeping shift in client age is more extensive than mere function. There is an additional audience growing in retiree education. Many retired seniors are sur-vivors of "the Great Depression" and then World War II. They have spent most of their lives trying to survive and now, they are indeed surviving—not just eco-nomically but age-wise as well. [3]At the turn of the millennium, senior citizens are more than a fifth of the American population and increasing. In fact the fast-est growing population segment is likely to be those over eighty five. In part because of lifestyle and in part because of safety nets, seniors are not only more affluent than their parents, but more physically active and politically aware. The Norman Rockwell picture of seniors rocking on the front porch is a fast fading memory. Today's seniors travel. They vote. *And they learn!* Senior style "universi-ties" are springing up so fast they are competing with traditional senior centers which tend to be day care for the immobilized. Senior courses include art, music, theater, philosophy, literature, estate planning, medical—even math and science. Many qualified universities include tuition free sequences leading to degrees.

They include physically disabled people but they are definitely not for the mentally disabled.

The retired population represents a very large new client base with brand new challenges for the school system. [3]They too require teaching methods, timing, and unusual locations convenient to them. Retirement homes, churches, conventional schools, senior centers, and even store fronts will become the new settings for education and openings for qualified teachers but the qualification requirements for teaching seniors will be very unique. Adolescents often tend to learn lessons as taught because their knowledge is too limited to challenge the material. Older people are less threatened, more experienced, and far more thought-provoking. It should make such classes more interesting for the instructors but the same teachers will need to accept dispute.

It sounds like a great deal of twenty-first century tempest for our national education system, but it is still not the end. [3]Women students already outnumber men and it would be a fair guess they will soon outnumber men in the workplace as well. They will have the identical need for continuous skill updates. Women were once the minority students of graduate schools but balance is already shifting. As more and more women enter the work place and many more enter professions, they will become the majority of post K-12 students. For an example in the 60's, men outnumbered women by more than twenty to one in law schools. As of the turn of the century, the split is about equal. Not only will their presence in the professions increase their attendance in the schools, but it will increase their political influence. For women, the quality of life has a greater urgency and the emphasis will encroach on curriculum, school funding, and school facilities, all of which will generate more demands on school systems for all ages. In part due to the increasing economic independence of women, the divorce rates will increase and the birthrate will decrease so teachers will need to deal with parents as separate entities in addition to their assigned charges. More of the instructor's time will be required, and as with all other careers, updated teaching training. It will probably require schools to teach pre-schoolers to learn before they ever get to grade school. The "day care" role will need to be abandoned to adapt a "day care/learning" function which will prepare the children of an increasingly erudite population of men and women to exceed their own parent's education. It also means maintaining American competitiveness in a global economy.

[3]This outcome will be supported by the emerging technological potential for many parents, and particularly women, to work at home. Home offices will permit women to actively monitor their children's progress in a much more critical manner than would have been the case if their sole occupation was home-

maker. Where such an option is not available, the growing number of dual income and single parent families will mandate company "day care learning centers" to enable corporate competition for high caliber employees. Even lower skill jobs, particularly those usually filled by women, will require day care learning facilities. All of this is new and very non-conventional schooling in the millennium!

The political diatribe for genuine universal educational advancement obscures an already incredibly complicated condition. Unfortunately, students come with varying abilities, language comprehension, cultural compatibility, and learning attitudes. The traditional teaching systems had, of necessity, to be based on an "average" student. The slow students were, in fact, left behind, while the brighter students were bored. Any new approach needs to accommodate those differences and in fact, there is current technology which is attempting to develop just such individualistic approaches.

[1]Computer learning software will permit students to receive personal instruction and progress at their own speed as needed. They can "fast forward" or repeat "classes" as determined by their performance. Students can be individually tested for competence with the computer, or his (or her) teachers or teacher's aid's proctoring the process. This allows observation of individual student performance *even if the student is not locally situated*. Assignments can be transferred to the computer and with interactive screens; the student is able to ask "questions" of the screen as a virtual instructor. Even more spectacular, in the not too distant future, voice synthesis might produce vocal screen response. As this system develops, and it will, one of the outstanding advantages will come to be the ability of the student or the instructor to choose both the question language and the response language in either written or vocal format. Such a system will go far in muting the demand for "multilingualism" which purportedly unfairly compromises the non-English speaking student's right to learn. Some suggest such a conversion will lead to the obsolescence of the "grade" school system and will really be individual instruction "par excellence" even for the non-average student.

This approach, if realized, has a number of interesting fringe effects with peculiarly new age facets. The requirements for an expansion in learning facility will enlarge the demand for new teacher training with new teaching skills and updated subject matter. In toto, they create a requirement for school building designs which do not even exist at this point. Computer education programs, of necessity, will tend to "universalize" curriculums. In an age of routine job migration, transferred children will be less disadvantaged by what might conceivably come to be frequent moves. In fact, those who do move might "remain" in their previous institution until semester completion via on-line classes. In addition, class size becomes a more muted subject because the student is essentially studying in his own space—i.e., the computer, so the absolute number of students in a room becomes less significant. Computer education furthermore tends to relieve the problem of school construction and therefore school budgets, because even storefronts can be used as classrooms in computer delivered courses. For students who are unable to attend "class" for reasons of weather or health, the on-line classroom transfers to the home with the Internet connection still permitting proctor participation.

[6]A major argument with this development is the claim students will need to have home computers in order to participate. This argument will very soon become hollow as conventional home TV sets are replaced with digital TV which opens a truly remarkable new world of added program services beyond entertainment. Digital TV will introduce a new type of TV accessory called "set top" boxes which permit ordinary TV sets to do much of the tasks more associated with PCs such as e-mail, Internet access, banking, bill payment, and the interactive school programming being described. [11]Set-top educational programs will permit students in different locations, indeed conceivably on different continents, to receive the same course material from the previously local source in an essentially classroom context. The set-top applications are already in development largely in anticipation of an expanding digital TV market. This is no longer a state of the art technology project. It is a marketing undertaking.

[6]Some argue that the system will teach reading but not reading books. Others respond with the equally valid argument that as many as one third of American school graduates are functionally illiterate, and it might be claimed the ability to read is, **sadly**, more important than the habit of reading books—already often lacking. Realistically speaking though, the electronic book is no longer an oncoming phenomenon. It's here, and decrying its presence is very much the same complaint which was heard when radio became widespread. This technology cannot be stopped and definitely can be positively employed to enhance the reading practice. It will, without question, become a publishing, not to mention distributor, revolution when cutting trees is no longer a prerequisite for publishing books. (Book publishers are considering how to deal with this competition.) There is no doubt something of intimacy is lost when the physical book is displaced but religious authorities in Gutenburg's time made the claim something was lost when just about anyone could pick up and read a book called "the Bible". The religions survived the printed bible, and the printed book will survive the electronic book.

Opening the student profile will become an active dynamic for how education is funded in the next decade. Home schooling, here-to-fore regarded as the private aberration of a few people, will probably become considerably more widespread for children because home office parents will be updating their own educations with computer delivered home study courses. The most valid contention with this mode argues that home study children don't experience the socializing influence of the public schools. The counter-argument is they can have a substantial socializing experience after school hours, in playgrounds, in churches, and in such institutions as the YMCA. Another claim points to competition of class peers which teaches children to cope with the competitiveness of the workplace. The counter—argument is the many studies which have shown that classroom children eventually learn their "position" in each class and often tend not to work beyond their own perception whereas the home schooled usually feel they are "special". There are many arguments pro and con for this proposition but the inescapable reality an increasing number of wage earners working and learning at home. More of the adolescent school population is sure to follow.

[5]Vouchers are an understandable twenty-first century exigency. This idea suggests that parent dissatisfied with their area public schools be given the option of enrolling their children in private schools, the costs for which would be partially provided by government funding. With twentieth century technology, there were basic supporting arguments for this alternative, the most formidable one being the provision of choices to low income students already available to wealthy ones. Still another market proven support for school choice is the concept of competition among schools. The principal of choice is arguably in sync with the times. However the ever present Law of Unintended Consequences is ever in operation. The flight of better students will not long be trailed by the flight of better administrators and educators. Better schools are notably partitioned from their under-performing brethren by wealth, to which problem vouchers would now add intellect, further disadvantaging the many left behind. The majority might additionally, and seriously, be damaged if school systems are forced to pay for those transfers via additional school taxes or lost funding.

[4]One would expect the principal of educational choice to result in forcing non-competitive schools or their non-performing teachers to "shape up" or close up. The experience with "free market" education is that the education market isn't open. The demand for educational resource is very large, but the supply is extremely limited. Few of the existing private schools are secular. Even allowing the principal of public funding for parochial purpose, a notion which has some very real constitutional problems, the number of available parochial school seats

is less than 5% of the current school population. The moneys withdrawn from public schools would significantly damage those institutions, because under-performing schools are most likely to be in under-funded neighborhoods while under-performing students invariably cost more to educate. Any conceivable benefit to the very few might be far outweighed by potential detriment to the very many.

[5]Supporters of voucher programs contend the vouchers can theoretically be used for any qualified institution; but the present certainty is almost all K-12 schools are religious. In Cleveland, Ohio, the hot current example, where there is actually a city approved voucher program which is being contested in the Supreme Court, over 96% of the voucher funds have been used in religious institutions. The Cleveland voucher stipend is insufficient to cover the costs of any of the city's secular schools so virtually none have agreed to accept voucher students. The same record indicates most of those now applying for voucher funds had, in any case, never before attended a public school so the program could conceivably end up being a money windfall for families which had "choice" without the program. Minority religious students, and presumably minority ethnic or racial students would, almost by definition, still have nowhere to go. As a matter of record, there is no evidence private schools with the same student profile do any better than the public institutions.

[5]Defenders of the existing system sometimes claim the critics are not sufficiently trained to judge the results. When they acknowledge problems at all, they attribute the cause to migrating jobs, to single parent households, or the minorities, or racism, or the welfare population, or our involvement with the outside world, or the intrusion of government, or senior citizen demands, or even Liberal "do-goodism". A pretty good case can be made for censure of each and every one of those listed and a great many others as well. However, given the dominating technological basis of the economy, the deficits of the school system simply won't await solution of all those problems and it is pretty safe to predict changes won't be long in coming. Curriculum, teacher's credentials, teacher's performance, teaching methods, teaching equipment, and certainly teaching hours will all be reviewed and revised.

[4]For example, there might be significant fringe benefits to longer school hours. (Studies have suggested "latchkey" children don't do as well, and tend to drop out of school more frequently.) At the very least, longer hours would gainfully occupy youngsters during a time slot many of them are otherwise unsupervised. (It is estimated as many as 7 million grade school children fall into that category and Department of Education believes that over a quarter million chil-

dren are actually homeless) Extending school hours might play a constructive day care role for many preschoolers in families whose finances preclude private day care learning institutions or better qualified baby sitters. A long term study conducted in Ypsilanti, Michigan, indicated that over two thirds of the attendees of Perry Preschool finished high school compared to less than half of those who did not. Less than a third of the yearlong preschoolers had subsequent police records while almost half of those who attended less than a year had some kind of record. This report is not so much an accolade for the Perry Preschool as it is for the principal of pre-schooling. Striking similarities have been found in the "Head Start" program. In addition to pre-schooling, initiating immigrant children into the English language and American culture would comprise another benefit of elongating school hours. It would appear the externalities of pre-schooling might save society more money than it cost.

[3][5]But without doubt, one of the great changes coming on will be in the concept of neighborhood schools funded by neighborhood taxes and programmed by neighborhood mores. This is a clearly nineteenth century construct based on the notion of neighborhoods which stably extended over many generations—an assumption which patently will no longer be operative. Future neighborhoods will be neither stable nor isolated from each other. What is different is that skilled worker shortages will threaten the middle class as well as the working class. What is singular is that dynastic wealth may no longer be guaranteed in this new economy. And what has changed is that education computerization will inevitably lead to national standards which will increasingly be funded by the state and federal governments. Federal, industrial, military, and even union involvement in local school budgets and in local scholarships will probably have many unforeseen consequences, but there are several which definitely can be anticipated. The local tax based motive underlying the principle of "local schools for local students" will have far less cogency as the definition of "local" changes. And the support of "vouchers" will lose some of its constituency as all the above comes into play.

With a number of acknowledged questions of consequence, computerized education will become more widespread, curriculum and teacher functioning will become more subject to comparison and competition. So the playing fields of educational institutions will become somewhat more level. Only in the ultimately modified circumstance of a more functional free school market, will it finally become difficult to reject the long experience that competition does energize improvements and innovation. The best record over time has been the element of competition and virtually everything we own and use today confirms the experience. In these two most sensitive areas of our lives, i.e., medical delivery and education delivery, competition has been impractical because of institutional structure. In many school systems, even individual merit pay increases are the exception while run of the mill institutions and personnel continue to receive support and tenure increases. *But*, if the adult student population increases according to forecast, the system will be dominated by tax paying citizens who will demand a tangible return on their personal investment, and by degrees, demand the same return on their tax investment in their children's education.

The options will come in many venues. Decreased localization is certainly the major prospect. The era of "school district" is probably drawing to a close. That would permit selection of schools even within the public domain. In fact, there are such experiments being conducted. The Minnesota system allows the parents to send their children to any public school in the state with the money following the children. The state even pays transportation costs. All the Minnesota schools might soon need to compete for their student body. Boston, Cambridge, and Fall River, all in Massachusetts, Montclair in New Jersey, and NYC district permit their children to go anywhere in the district. Iowa even allows children to attend out of state schools. Arkansas, Iowa, Nebraska, Ohio, and Wisconsin all have pilot programs in place. It is a bit early for results to be tabulated but some early trends are already appearing. In Cambridge, after many years of frustrations, the SAT average is up by 90 points. Montclair New Jersey scores have also shown some marked upward movement. East Harlem's District IV has over 40% of its students making it to school each day with 90% graduating.) Only 64% read at grade level but it started at 15%. The negative side of a competitive school system might include new job descriptions such as public relations officers and advertising budgets because school competition, like industrial competition, is a race for customers.

Another suggestion being considered would have a local university site-manage area schools. [6] This idea is actually being attempted in Massachusetts. The Chelsea school system is being managed by Boston University. [5]Public aid to private schools established in inner city areas is still another experiment. It sounds like a voucher program but it is associated with the school itself, rather than its' enrollment. In fact, many private universities, perhaps most, are already receiving public moneys in the form of grants or endowments. If the size of the grant were somehow linked to the number of minority students achieving measurable goals, the students would actually become a measurable asset.

Industrial involvement with the education process is not new. What is new is the rate at which it is growing. The activity is budding in several patterns. Most

American based Japanese companies are actually known for their in-house training programs. [6]Many American corporations have regularly operated in-plant schooling facilities to train their employees to company standards. Whenever necessary, for instance in strongly ethnic communities, they also taught Basic English and cultural content as well. But commercial corporations are recognizing the long term skill deficit as a threat to their own future and are directly supporting particular schools. General Electric, for example, is a sponsor for the Manhattan Center for Science and Mathematics. The Polaroid Corporation sponsors a program for teacher training at Harvard. The American Express Co. sponsors finance training programs in a number of American high schools. It is probably no exaggeration to say that virtually every major corporation endows teaching positions at some school.

As a clarion note to this trend it should be noted that the key to any such programs of the future will lie in the new icon of the times, information. In order for the government (or the sponsor) to track results, and to enable the parents to make choices, public accounting will need to be made concerning facilities, personnel, qualifications, programs, and, most important, an accurate accounting of actual accomplishments. They will be very sweeping indeed. There is already a considerable industry in university rating books because colleges not only compete for students, but for the money the students bring to the school. As private adult re-training schools proliferate, similar rating systems will propagate to fill this very important niche. And as the constituency of "K-12" choice becomes more widespread those institutions will experience the same need to demonstrate both credentials and performance. Schools which reject rating will suffer student, and financial loss. Furthermore, subjecting themselves to rating will inevitably force them to homogenize courses and teacher qualifications to national standards. That will also add to the pressure for reducing local syllabus proclivity.

Projecting an increasing level of individual educational selectivity does not imply there won't be concurrent problems. The concept will not be as radical in the twenty-first century as it was in the twentieth but there are some very valid objections to open school choice programs, the most obvious being it would materially alter the school busing program and might therefore affect the school desegregation policy. In one of the many turnabouts of history, it might turn out that inner city schools which become competitive will not lose students to suburban schools which would substantively extend the life of "minority majority" schools. This would become a case of balancing priorities and if such programs were potentially successful, the long term alternatives would be better education or expanded integration—not an easy pick. Furthermore, the Supreme Court ruled in the Brown decision schools segregated by race are "inherently" inferior. Given that decision, it is at the very least implied the nation might eventually find that schools segregated by economics or ethnicity are also inferior. There is little doubt that the millennium will eventually address that condition, searching for alternatives most prominent of which will be computerized instruction.

The United States scored close to the bottom of a series of multinational studies of student knowledge of math and science. The most recent report came from the Third International Mathematics and Science Study released in 1998. Even the American top level students scored pretty close to the bottom of the tested nations with Europeans generally scoring at or near the top of the twenty one nations tested. This should come as no surprise. Half a century ago Americans were generally satisfied with their own school system whereas in more recent polls Americans ranked education reform as close to their top issue. Americans have recognized the problem without polls and tests. Whatever the "fix", the pressure from the people is to do something and do it fast.

Summary:

Having generated the most creative surge of applied technology in history, America is in the odd position of making obsolete the school system which produced it. Even though the achievements of the various remedial approaches and experiments are not yet apparent, there are certainly common perceptible trends to all of them. Decentralizing school systems, which is an underpinning to all of these innovations, will reduce dependence on local school taxes which inevitably will tend to equalize school systems in terms of cost per student, teacher qualifications, and teaching methodology. Detachment will require substitute moneys from both state and federal sources. Disconnect from local funding will promote standardized curriculums and standard outcome evaluations, and those strategies will heavily depend on computer equipment for teacher support and outreach systems. In this last regard there will be some less obvious fringe effects. It takes many years for school books to be approved and then they need to be cost effective. Texas and California are the major purchasers of school texts with the result that anyone writing a new text needs to be certain the book will meet the approval of the Texas and California system without which textbook costs would be prohibitive. It's just basic business accounting. This extends the "writing" sequence and contributes to a chronic condition of obsolete books. Many books now in use in some school systems still refer to the "Soviet Union" as a current fact of life. As an alternative, computer accessible online books are relatively cost free and can be updated literally instantly and cost effectively, and can even be used selectively. They may age out, but they don't wear out. The equipment requires an investment but it is independent of grade level and can be programmed for special tutorial assistance. It is very regrettable today's youngsters are far more adjusted to receiving information via video sources than through print but that must certainly, in the context of this subject, be a significant further advantage of desk-top learning.

Conformity was a traditionally pervasive school administrative requirement. Orthodoxy will become a diminishing policy. Passive acceptance of a non-functional system could only occur when the results of the break down were delayed in effect—i.e., when there was a time lapse between the time of learning and the time of application. In this new era, the adult students enrolled in an ongoing retraining system will demand rapid results because they or their employers will very likely personally be paying part or all of the bills. Their own expectation of a positive learning result will certainly be translated into determination for equivalent performance for their children's schools. If such correspondence doesn't happen the reaction will be apparent at the registrar's office or the ballot box.

Beyond all the physical and technical requirements of this unprecedented time of expansion, the need most difficult to fill will be the human element. Whatever else becomes available by public decision, without incentive, the potential teachers will only enter the field by personal choice. As of this point there is little if any incentive to choose teaching as a career. Parents often see them as a form of babysitter. They are expected to adapt to the cultural and language variations of particular districts. Teachers are faulted for inadequate attention to individual students when the average class size is somewhere between thirty and forty students. They are held responsible for poor school functioning in a system designed to discourage innovation. They are accused of being excessively political in a system which is dominated by politicians. Hardly least of the teacher's problems, is the new age mobility of the parents. Lifetime jobs are a thing of the past with job tenure shrinking. Teachers are never certain their student compliment at the end of the semester will be who it was at the beginning. With no national educational standards, the students might be forced to transfer, but their achievement status is left behind. And with all of that, teacher salaries largely depend not on their individual performance or credentials but rather on the area in which they teach. Over-all they are underpaid in any comparison to most other professionals with their level of education. As an example, starting engineers are paid about fifty percent above what starting teachers get.

To say that the availability of teaching talent is inadequate to need in this field which is likely to double over the next quarter twenty five years, is reckless understatement. This situation is so serious many, probably most, school districts have taken to using unqualified or less qualified "volunteers" to fill out the teaching staff. Many of these volunteers have educations related to the subject they teach but they have neither teaching training nor certification and with all the best intentions, are not subject to supervision because they are "volunteers". Few of them are willing to operate in inner city schools where the need is greatest, for the obvious reason they rarely live there. At least twenty states have approved some version of "alternative certification" to try to fill this void. Nice try, but no cigar. Very few actually expect stopgap measures of this kind will even dent the shortage problem and teacher's organizations view such policies, with some justification, as an additional threat to their professional status. The simple truth is the millennial pastures are much greener elsewhere.

There will be other even more substantial threats to professional teacher status, not the least of which is their need to somehow introduce multi-cultural American concepts into subjects such as civics courses for students with no prior exposure to diversity. They are expected to engage gender neutral classroom activities to ethnic male centered students without offending either the students or their parents. They are required to extol the virtues of separation of church and state to students who have been taught their church *should be the state*. All of that with little or no guidance from politically sensitive school authorities who have notably less experience with such circumstance than do the teachers.

The education plant of the millennium is facing situations which were never envisioned by any prior generation, certainly not by the founding fathers of the Republic who established the initial thrust for public education. The teachers are at the forefront of this revolution with little real guidance and less situation training. In response, many states are belatedly passing teacher "competency" requirements which include subject specific majors and education minors as well as diversity training. All of this will have an unintended outcome of further separating local education from local control. All of it will tend to further diminish the share of educational costs underwritten by real estate taxes. All of it will increasingly require performance evaluations of the students, of the teachers, and perhaps most important, of institutional administrations. And for all of those reasons, all of it will be resisted by all concerned. With their occupation's principles changing so fast, the teaching profession will develop accountability standards and functions very similar to the Bar Association or the Medical

Association but they will also have achieved the professional status they deserve, as well as the salaries appropriate to their professions.

Following the course of this discussion might suggest the next era's schools should be concentrating on university and professional level job training but that is not exclusively the case. It is true that technology advance demands technical competence. There was a time, only recently, when inadequately educated students could find jobs on farms, and even in factories. Training has always been the key to advancement, but now, it has virtually become the key to survival. Low skill or repetitive jobs are being steadily replaced by automation or export. No laws, no unions, no corporate policy, and indeed, no good intentions will change this progression. However, the distinction between professions and trades does not necessarily imply a correspondence between trade skills and no skills. Unlike the past, job training, like professional training, will become an inescapable lifetime activity. As technology continues to transform products and process, most of the likely trade schools will probably be private or industrial—an outcome which manifestly promotes competition. Many—perhaps most—blue collar jobs will also require some level of training in abstract problem solving using both math and language skills. Twenty-first century trade schools will need to feature high tech industrial subjects including operation and maintenance of digital equipment like computers and computer machine controls, automation process, medical gear, contamination and pollution control. Learning to learn on an ongoing basis will become a priority subtext of every course. Trade schools will need to maintain much greater liaison with *anticipated* industrial needs to keep their students current. Schools will need to promote that recognition by also having courses designed to train students of both the trades and the professions to anticipate opportunities on the horizon as early as possible. Secretaries, who spotted the advent of word processing, were suddenly in high demand when desk top computers began to appear in the 80's.

Furthermore, the volatility of new age jobs will make self-employment more attractive than ever. At this time specialized training is particularly appropriate to entrepreneurial students who will need to learn the basics of marketing, sales, accounting, money management, and fund raising, as well as hands on business planning. It's a condition the schools are already beginning to deal with and will be forced to formally address much more seriously. Virtually every large industrial community of the 1980s was impacted by corporate downsizing with very serious losses of long standing jobs and tax income. Many long time citizens were forced to migrate to find alternative employment. For those who remained, the substitute sometimes turned out to be free lance work. Towns like Buffalo, N.Y.,

Pittsburgh, Pa., Philadelphia, Pa., and New York City, have set up courses specifically aimed at self employment. In many of them direct small business work experience is actually part of the educational process. The entire world is becoming a single marketplace and while the professions and the trades will certainly continue to expand, opportunities for small business will flare in America.

This is obviously going to be a pioneering period. The information age will be even more complicated. The large increase in adult student body, contributing at least in part, to the costs of their ongoing education, will generate many unconventional needs. A sizeable portion of the increase will be minority groups, some of which will be serious cultural misfits in an information age. It's an age of the most extensive human relocations on the books and the mix is ongoing and churning. Many transplants, already uprooted from their own background, feel that modern education further alienates their children from their origins. Even among native born Americans, farm upbringing, regional conditions, religious persuasions, poverty, single parent backgrounds, all inhibit performance in the best schools with the best equipment and instruction. In prior times they could find work in new factories, but in this era manufacturing jobs will continue to decline while service industries take up more than three quarters of the available national jobs. Knowledge workers will constitute more than half of the operating jobs. More women will enter the work force and many more immigrants. All of that will substantially alter the content of education.

And we are still not the end. In the context of the American economy, a federal education policy will become linked as a national security policy. And it will require education policy associated with very new goals. Furthermore, in spite of substantial salary improvements, teachers will actually need increased, possibly mandated, parental participation at least in part because there will be less local administrative input. The diversity of the next decades combined with Internet connectivity, will make parental involvement more effective but also make it more necessary.

That inevitable total process will generate a great deal of heat because of unintended consequence. National policy will be forced by global pressures to set minimum doctrine for secular subjects such as math, science, literacy, etc., diverting the assets of any partially funded religious institutions from their primary purpose, and probably inadvertently undermining enrollment. At the same time, the expanding demand will generate an open market place and there is no doubt a major part of the educational market is going to be secular private institutions of grade school level all the way through, and including, retirement, with non-government facilities, staff and private finances. In order to compete, these institutions will need to have schedules and programs adapted to the needs of their clients which translate to non-traditional hours and content. They will be another source of pressure on the public and parochial school systems to break with the confines of history. Industry makes priority verdicts as to market requirements so corporations will share in the metamorphosis. Corporations don't make open ended investments. They too will stipulate standardized content and measurable results and that constraint will overflow from corporate schools to both public and private schools of any category. If corporate sponsored school instructors produce outstanding results, they will be paid outstanding salaries. If a new technology attracts customers, that technology will appear in the classroom. Under-performers, teachers or students, will not long be tolerated and that too will seriously alter public school practice.

Using any criteria, the established American education system was already inadequate during the machine age and is actually archaic for the information age. Education will become a lifetime activity and learning to learn will become a major subject. All the school systems—public, private, and industrial—will be forced to interact and coordinate as an ongoing fact of life which forecasts national teaching and learning standards. The teaching industry, and that certainly is what it will become, will need to apply a level of professional diversity never before considered which means schools of all descriptions will need to constantly update equipment, course content, and culture. In short schools will need to constantly revise their basic product in exactly the same manner, and for the same reasons as their industrial equivalents.

[7] Alex de Tocqueville's nineteenth century commentary on American society predicted that "What the few have today, the many will demand tomorrow." That astonishingly accurate observation previews the American potential for a high technology culture. In an information based society, the dead weight of social class will be more likely to give way to the advantage of knowledge so the disadvantage of poverty will likely be considerably less defining than has been the historic case. Tocqueville's tomorrow is our today. If the American system of education improves its performance, Tocqueville's description will be graphically demonstrated in the twenty-first century.

Reading and Reference:

[1] *Religion and Change* D.L.Edwards

[2] *Shopping for Faith* Cimino & Lattin

[3] *Schools of the Future* Marvin Cetron 0 07 010350 X

[4] Educational Futures Sourcebook Kierstead, Bowman, Dede

[5] *Education Vouchers from Theory to AlumRock* Mecklenburger & Hostrop 0 88280 002 7

[6] *Educational Renaissance* Cetron & Gayle 0 312 05422

[7] *The Contest for Educational Resources Weaver* 0 669 04586 1

[8] *Cheating Death* The Promise and the Future Impact of Trying to Live Forever. Cetron & Owens 0 312 18065 9

[9] *Newsweek* January 1, 2000

[10] *Civilizing the Internet* J.M.Kizza 0 7864 0539 2

[11] *The Essential Guide to Digital Set-top Boxes & Interactive TV* G.O'Driscoll 0 13 017360 6

[12] *IEEE Spectrum* August, 1998

6

Jobs—The Affluent Gypsies

There once was a cartoon called "the Little King" in which the Prime Minister informs the king that "the peasants are revolting" to which the king responds despondently, "I know, I know". The king was out of touch with his time. Pre-Euro Union twentieth century Europeans, on the other hand, were often, in touch with their time, but out of touch with their future. Good times, they said, were the discontinuities between bad times. In post war WWII), America, recessions were becoming the "adjustments" between prosperous times. It's easy to fall into the trap of here and now, and nowhere will such disconnect with the future hit home with more repercussion than the workplace. It's might seem Panglossian to project an ebullient America in the midst of a recession and a war on terrorism, but in terms of the real job outlook for the age of information, optimism is the more appropriate outlook.

For ten thousand years, much of what people valued most were physical "things"—Land—gold—machines—water—all "things". Possessions were our goals and our status symbols. We even lusted for them. More than anything else, we worked for them. Ownership of things gave us security, and comfort. Most of the wisdom of history was ultimately directed toward acquisition or production of those "things". And of course, our corporations earned their returns by marketing "things". Whatever services they performed was largely as support for the "things' they produced.

Now, for the first time in our long history, intellectual production has become more valuable than the physical goods we produce and the transformation is being reflected in the working world. There are lots of obvious examples. The Colonel doesn't sell chicken sandwiches, he sells franchises. The cable companies rent cable converters only in order to rent cable service. Even the General Electric Company's focus business is financial service. Ford and GM will soon be producing their annual corporate profit from onboard service connection to GPS and mobile telephones. Jobs and salaries invariably follow profits and it is already abundantly clear the best individual rewards will not be on the factory floor. The ideal for the most valuable employee has shifted from being "hard working" to being "creative" and the shift signals a new game plan of the workplace.

Concurrent with this revision of corporate emphasis is the metamorphosis from a national to an international economy which further magnifies the workplace uncertainty. Robert Reich, the Harvard economist, made that point over a decade ago, in his book "The Work of Nations" when he pointed out that "knowledge rather than national boundaries defines today's developed markets" and those markets drive the workplace. Few dispute global commerce as a net benefit to the nation as a whole, but there are losers. In short terms, the winners will be the trained and the trainable, and of course, always the wealthy. The losers will be everyone else. The digital economy causing all the changes is still in its infancy but already the number of new industries, new opportunities,—and, incidentally, new threats—are impressive. Most of them did not exist ten years ago. People with the current skills and training are likely to earn more income than most of them anticipate.

The key component of "workplace" has conventionally been the notion of "place". Unions were chartered on it. Benefits were founded on it. [10]Entire towns, families, and lifestyles were planned around it. Even taxes were predicated on the presence of local plants. The "company town" became commonplace as did father and son jobs. With this revised economy, physical products are being downgraded on the economic food chain, demoting factories along with their physical location. "Company town" is now mostly a cross word term. Even shipping distance is of secondary concern because the weight and volume of most modern products is often so negligible the instruction book is heavier than the product. If you are skeptical, check your cell phone. The whole world is becoming a common business venue so the prime concern of corporations will likely be politics rather than location.

[1][7]Career jobs will become an ebbing vestige of a dead age. Technology certainly creates new jobs, but in doing so it also eliminates old jobs and old locations. (It's called "selective destruction") Perceptions of "home town", church, and group loyalties will become more uncertain. Unions will have a diminished role in the job market, and, collaterally, on the political scene. But most of all it will change the basis of career planning.

At least half of all jobs already require more than a high school education. [2]Among the occupations the Bureau of Labor Statistics (the BLS) projects to grow the fastest over the next decade, virtually all are occupations which will require either education or training beyond high school. And again, even among the winners, those dealing directly with knowledge will generally do better than those relating to "things". The BLS projections make this point very impressively. Over the period of 1998 to 2008, computer analysts will double technical engineering, science employment will grow as much as 43%, and executive and management employment by as much as 20%. Even engineering technicians are expected to expand their numbers by almost 20%. In contrast, materials engineers will only increase by 9%, nuclear engineers by 6%, while industrial production management, considered the prince of engineering in the age of factories, is actually expected to contract. All farm related jobs, including farm managers are expected to decrease. Mining engineering and even petroleum engineering are both expected to dwindle.

[2]Symptomatically, the greater the job objective, the higher will be the required education. The number of jobs requiring an Associate Degree or higher already accounted for 25% of all jobs in 1998, and they will grow to 40% of all *available* jobs. That is twice as fast as the average job growth and most of the new jobs requiring a degree will pay much higher than the average for all jobs.

Before the Civil War this was an agricultural nation and what opportunity existed was largely related to land. As manufacturing grew during the 20th century, agriculture faded. Today, agriculture is less than 3% of the U.S. labor force. But today, manufacturing itself is shrinking in terms of its' share of the American economy and in terms of total employment. [2]Though still about 30% of total GDP, manufacturing jobs are actually expected to decline by about a third of a million jobs over the next decade alone. This phenomenon has been given a name. It's called the "hollowing of American industry". So an automatic lathe operator, who was on top of the industrial heap only a decade ago, will probably in due course be replaced by a high school student who can "wipe" a machine program card through the machine card reader. [1][10]As a matter of record, today's products take less than 40% of the blue collar labor time the same product took only 25 years ago. Producing "things" is definitely not the optimum career plan at this new point in time.

Still, America will not become a nation of key clickers. Cohen and Zysman wrote a book called "Manufacturing Matters" in which they effectively make the point that manufacturing always matters, and indeed it does. [11]A nation lacking in production capacity is not only economically exposed, it is also militarily vulnerable. As an equally compelling point, the so-called "military-industrial complex" is usually the driving energy for the technologies of the information era and such origins definitely includes both the computer and the Internet. Information technologies not only originate production line efficiencies, they also improve information access efficiencies. This is so true that the age has been alternately named the "Age of Connectivity" or the "Age of Access". In the context of our subject of the moment, what it will mean in practical terms is that the sale of products will be displaced by the sale of information services associated with those products. Good examples are plentiful. Software companies Microsoft and Intuit for example, routinely discount initial installation costs in order to gain permanent customers for add-on services. Banks will provide free on-line banking PC programs. Furniture companies are renting entire pre-decorated suites of furnishings because the likely renewals generate more profits than one time furniture sales. Companies with patents are licensing the entire production process out to "generic" producers because the strategy minimizes capital requirements and generates post patent profits. Every hardware chain uses tool rentals as a growing source of profitability and customer base expansion.

What all of them are doing is using products to develop long term commercial relationships with customers rather than generating their profit from spot sales of products. [5]The transaction of importance is a continuous service association. In such strategies, expanding literally every day, the physical product is reduced to a sales aid. If you are renting a Buick, your next rental is likely to be another Buick. What all of them get is extended (and extensive) access to their customer's personal habits, preferences, and even their financial behavior. What comes along with long term inter-active relationships is intimate knowledge of individual customer lifestyles and tastes. It's more than just good public relations, in this coming service economy it will be good marketing.

[2]The BLS projections reflect the new economic picture. They expect advertising, marketing and public relations jobs to increase by over 20% over the next ten years. They forecast product demonstrators and product promoters to increase by 32%—and *service* sales representatives by an astonishing 51%—those being over half a million jobs in just those three categories alone. With manufactured products being relegated to a support role, production plants and their workers have similarly reduced consequence to corporate planning. Again, as illustrations, the BLS projections expect expansions in factory machinists to be a modest 6% over the decade, metalworking about 3%, welders about 8%, and even blue-collar supervisors, only 9%. When it comes to the textile and apparel industry, the outlook gets downright grim. Over the next decade the apparel working cadre will drop by 17%, shoe and leather workers by 18%, and textile machinery operators by 19%

[2]Inverse with the factory numbers shrinkage, the service component of this equation increases steadily, as does their personal income potential. The contrast

with the same companies' information workers has to be impressive. Over the corresponding period of 1998 to 2008, accountants are expected to increase by 11%, administrative services by 18%, marketing personnel by 23%, management analysts by 28% and information engineers by a whopping 43%. The implication to be drawn here is that jobs producing physical products, regardless of training, skill, or even education, are, in general, declining in number and significance in the coming decade. Jobs dealing with information are increasing in total and in importance.

The key components of this stage are education and job mobility. This process is not a matter of politics or policy. It's not a "conspiracy "of the rich and the educated". Like machinery in the industrial age, mobility is an unconditional feature of the information age. Laws can't stop it. Unions won't change it. And populist opposition is self defeating. One way or another we will all need to learn to live with it. But the pay-off for the dilemma is greatly increased returns to more people than ever before.

[2]Having made so much of "mobility", the health delivery industry will really be unique. Its' most singular feature is a market that far exceeds predictable resources for the foreseeable future. Its' customer base is geographically as well as demographically escalating. As long as most of the population of the world can't afford health services, those who can will probably be compelled subsidize those who can't. Few places in the world are more than hours away from anywhere else and in this age of mass transportation and travel, diseases cannot be quarantined within any borders. AIDS, a disease which erupted two decades ago in Africa, has become the greatest threat to the physical and economic health of the entire globe since the Bubonic Plague. Curing AIDS is no longer a requisite of compassion. It has become a prerequisite for the stability of the world and therefore an acknowledged target of American technology and foreign policy.

The medical field has many other distinctions which make it a particularly singular workplace. In an age where products obsolete so fast manufacturers need to issue serial numbers to establish a product's generation, the stethoscope and the aspirin of generations are still current. Medical technology is racing but this is one field where the new builds on, but retains much of the old. Medical equipment represents such a large investment of finance and facility, resources replacement is generally not feasible except with time. Write-off of almost any equipment requires its operation for as long as it is medically valid, which is usually the equipment lifetime. Some operating and useful X-Ray equipment are older than the technician. While new equipment always means updated training, another parameter, forced by economics and enabled by microprocessors, is ever simplifying operation. By and large, very sophisticated "smart" medical equipment is intended to be operated successfully by technicians.

[2]So, in the context of the coming working condition, the medical workplace will be almost extraordinary as regards *job longevity, and location stability.* The BLS projections testify eloquently as regards job availability in this career. They expect increases in the order of 20% or more for Chiropractors, Physicians, Registered Nurses, Dietitians, and even Veterinarians. BLS anticipates some truly impressive non-physician job market performance as well. For instance, Occupational Therapists and Physical Therapists—will grow 34%; Physicians Assistants—up 47%; Respiratory Therapists—up 43%; and Speech and Language Therapists—up 38%. Therapists seem to be the real winners during this immediate period.

[2]On a somewhat lower training level, but still impressive, they expect increases in the order of 10 to 20% or more for Optometrists and Opticians, Podiatrists, Pharmacists, and Medical Laboratory technicians. Included in the percentage growth anticipation are Cardio-vascular technicians, Pharmacy technicians, Paramedics, Practical Nurses, and virtually all the other medical technician fields. To recognize the medical field as a growth field in the 21st century is really missing the mark. We are speaking of hundreds of thousands of new—and stable—jobs with growing career potential, and all this is for just the United States market! Nevertheless, salaries will usually reflect training and education.

The enlargement of the health care industry is so compelling it has become part of the national political agenda. Health related services actually dominates the list of growth industries and will be a priority for both major political parties. The industry has been growing faster than the GNP ever since World War II when the military were forced to research health care in a much more systematized manner as a military consideration. Patient expectations for "cure-alls" and "miracle cures" have exceeded even the growth of this flourishing industry. It didn't take very long for the health market dimensions to reach insurance companies. Medical insurance, which started as a retirement advantage for U.S. military veterans, will soon be considered an "entitlement" of all citizens. Medical insurance equates to more medical jobs.

[2]Some specialty fields with relatively lower qualifications requirements such as on-the-job type training or company provided training, also look pretty good in the context of future growth. Among such fields are home health care aides—58% increase; security guards—29% increase; vending machine repair—16% increase; roofers—12% increase; taxi drivers—20% increase; and

truck drivers—15% increase; Their consideration here is relative job and location stability, and very important in this category, probable union protection.

Finally, there will be many growing job opportunities in the service sector at entry levels as for instance in such positions as billing and file clerks, order clerks, landscaping, grounds keeping, lawn service, and generally in food preparation and delivery. In many such vocations, education will not be a serious factor although even here, it helps. In some of those callings there are both blue collar and white collar jobs which will actually grow in number and in salary because high tech automation is increasing productivity and incidentally, they too are the types of occupations which cannot be moved at all, much less moved off shore. The advantage for these kinds of jobs is that automation will reduce the weight of direct labor as a cost factor probably allowing for improved salary conditions.

[1][6]There are additional reasons why industrial employment will continue to drop as a percentage national employment. Unions tend to blame off-shore sources for this continuing slide but much of the manufacturing being done in third world countries in the past was low skill, repetitive work with little, if any, hope for advancement and even less real prospect for duration. It is the kinds of work American plants are trying to shed and that union membership will increasingly recognize as hopeless. It's not that it doesn't have a future. It doesn't even have a present. Nike, the largest footwear company in the world doesn't own any plants at all. They actually order all their products from overseas and merely resell them. Even for the off-shore companies, cheap labor is a very self-deluding advantage because eventually the "smart machines" will replace even the cheapest labor and repetitious operation is the most easily automated. At the same time, social pressure in industrializing third world nations will drive their wages up as is happening in Mexico, China, and elsewhere.

[2]For the recent past, most of the job growth and virtually all of the better job growth has been in service industries. Buying a product is different in its essence from buying a service. Buying a product leaves the customer with property. Buying a service leaves him with nothing. Even so, it's important to recognize the high tech service sector, i.e., the "intellectual services", as a major contributor to the growth in the low tech service sector. In a household where all the adults work, most of the labor, once done by family is now being farmed out. Childcare and house maintenance are now a day temp industry. Pre-cooked meals, once unthinkable, and restaurants, once a social event, are now both routine events. Indeed, in spite of the great proliferation of fast food and ethnic dining places, salad bars, and deli's, it is almost rare to get a table without waiting. This is so common that an entire industry has emerged for producing electronic

paging devices to alert the customer that his table is ready. In fact, all this dining out has led to a boom in entry level restaurant jobs.

The same circumstances has led to another boom in childcare centers with something approaching a quarter million jobs being projected to be created within the next decade. Indeed, this is another driving source for the demand for pre-schooling. In a rather unexpected outcome, two income families have contributed to the meteoric growth of home health care services. Within the memory of many present day caretakers, care of the aged was culturally a family responsibility. "Farming them out" to commercial nursing homes and day care personnel would have been something of a stain on the family reputation. Not any more. Still, although the jobs in this industry are growing, the US Dept. of Commerce reports many working poor are care providers so that at this point, patient care taking is not a good career plan for ambitious people. "Entry level" jobs in any industry are exactly what the name implies except that this particular type of job very rarely outgrows its' initial conditions.

[8]With some real motion sickness ups and downs, e-commerce is clearly coming into its own because it serves the widening double income family market and the rising senior citizen demand. Disabled people, busy people, people in remote places, even people in third world countries can all access this market. While it is still finding its' legs, the fact is e-commerce will very soon make big business sense and here too workers with only moderate training will find increasing employment and some opportunity for growth. So, it is clearly in service industries where the action, the future, and the real money lie. According to the U.S. Chamber of Commerce, within the next decade, nearly half of all American workers will be employed in industries which either use, or produce information as a primary output.

Nobody is more startled by the speed at which information technology has grown than the computer industry which gave birth to it. It took almost three centuries for the industrial revolution to take over the Western world. Information technology has taken over virtually the entire world in less than three decades. The Internet is possibly the most powerful human macrocosm ever produced. Already, the Internet generates as much annual revenue—while not yet profitable—after only a decade as the automobile industry produces after a century. It took thirty eight years for 30% of households to acquire a telephone; seventeen years for a television receiver, but only seven years for 30% of households to connect to the Internet. In 1995 there were about twenty two million Internet subscribers. In the millennial year 2002, the estimate is well over one hundred and thirty million subscribers.

[2]The job market created by the information upheaval is changing too fast to precisely describe except as a snapshot in time. Actual employment in the personal computer industry has dropped since the 1980s but this decrease has been almost balanced by job growth associated with microprocessor control development. Before the year 2000 recession you could pick up any newspapers employment section and the ads for programmers, Web designers, language analysts, data base specialists, computer enhancement specialists, or, for that matter, *any* computer related specialty—fill in the blank—and the help wanted ads didn't fill columns, they filled pages and as often as not, entire separate sections. In spite of the current downturn of the economy and the international outsourcing of jobs, the majority of think tanks attentive to this field forecast a near term return to that circumstance. Witnesses before Congressional hearings testified that the envisioned shortage of trained people for this field will continue for at least **the next quarter century**, in spite of any relatively short term economic cycles. Indeed, they testified those shortages were a menace facing this industry.

[2]Unlike the previous "low tech" jobs which industry usually produces, these jobs will demand very high skills commonly requiring at least a college degree (the Hudson Institute survey Workforce 2000 estimates more than 52% of *all* millennial jobs will require at least some college education) and many of them will demand post graduate degrees as well. All of them require constant updating of skills. Information professionals, much like medical professionals, never "finish" their education. The personal investment is large, but the return on investment is likely to be even larger. U.S. Dept. of Labor reports that real salaries (i.e., including adjustments for inflation) in this industry have grown by 19% over the last decade compared to an average 5% for the rest of the private sector and start off salaries in this sector fair better than 78% above the private sector averages. As noted, post recession, the pattern is expected to continue for the next quarter century even including recessions.

[12][13]The long term employment deficit is resulting in some real forward thinking within the industry. The advent of communications satellites, the Internet, the cell phone, the video phone, the pagers, voice recognition, unique keyboards, etc., is permitting revolutionary labor practices to succeed operationally. It will soon be perfectly possible, in fact simple, to connect PC's, and interactive digital television sets from any location to the corporate system which means people will work out of their homes, their cars, and even out of airplanes and remain in constant contact, including conferences, orders, catalogs and all the other paraphernalia of any business operation. It will permit the hiring of disabled but otherwise qualified personnel, people with family responsibilities, inaccessible

people, and particularly senior citizens. That will allow flexible schedules and even task splitting. It will reduce the potential for job and gender discrimination, and as a result of all of the above, will reduce operating costs because non-office employees will reduce the need for corporate brick and mortar.

But everything has a price. (During his jury summation in the "monkey trial", Clarence Darrow is reported to have said "man will learn to fly, but the clouds will smell of gasoline"). New technologies always have a down-side. Perhaps the most unpredicted negative of the digital transformation is a very short product market life. Rapid product obsolescence is a grave concern for union workers. Unions have done best in mass production industries such as construction, automotive, and appliances. These "big ticket" fabricators are specifically the kinds of enterprises which are losing out in this new service environment. Such products are classified as "durable goods" because they were expected to last over three years. But the market life of most products is far shorter. Any computer you buy at an outlet is, by the conditions of this market, obsolete as you take it home. As the product market life cycle shortens the work sources will increase their mobility. The old IBM truism—"I'll Be Moving"—will become a millennial workplace axiom. Renting homes will become more practical than owning them reversing over a hundred years of government policy. Already more than a third of all American automobiles produced are rented. Modern technologies minimize distance as a planning factor. Plants can be relocated easily and controlled remotely. A digitized process controlled from an office, does not in any way limit where the office is located. In the case of Nike, the controlling office could be 13,000 miles away.

[2]Finding lifetime jobs will be problematical. Process and tools will be revised so often skills will be short-lived. And even if you're looking for professional stability, you're unlikely to find it. For information professionals, this will not be much of an employment problem since the next job is only a telephone call away, and they can often operate out of their homes. But for lower level workers, and even many skilled technicians, such an environment will likely become a concern involving family and homes, as well as many other financial and emotionally painful issues. For the unions this means more fluid membership at the very least and, unless their basic strategy changes, less political clout.

Unlimited connection will also tend to increase working hours, although those hours might be spent in the home. Home offices, particularly remote home offices will also muddle fringe benefit compensation—medical as an example. They will likely complicate legal considerations as well. If, for example, you fall down in your own workplace home, *during working hours* (itself a hazy legal definition), is the employer liable under Workman's' Compensation or the Occupational Safety and Health Administration (OSHA) laws? If either Workman Compensation or OSHA regulations apply to your home, the government might have the right to come into your home for safety inspection purposes. Whose will be the responsibility for an injured social visitor—or your wife—in the working home? In the age when someone is to be blamed for anything untoward, where a lady sued McDonalds because she ordered a cup of hot coffee—and got a cup of hot coffee, this will be neither a simplistic nor a funny question. It would not be much of a theoretical extension to consider the legal implications of home offices where the employer disallows private parties where drinking takes place. And almost in the realm of surrealism, whose will be the responsibility for any illegal activity if you are under home employment contract to a number of different employers at the same time? If you are laughing, you might be interested to know that all of the above are actually being considered.

[10]There are more immediate aspects of the millennial work place (wherever it may be) which also requires mention. Personal privacy issues are on the increase for some very practical reasons. If employees routinely have corporate sponsored access to the Internet (of course it automatically carries over from office to home or on the road), are their personal e-mails entitled to mail privacy law? If employers will be paying for home communications, will the employee be entitled to normal privacy in using those communications? Automatic messages warning of "monitored" phone conversations are now common. Technology already exists to monitor lines but it goes even further for the employers of "at-home" employees. If you use on-line-banking for keeping your personal financial records, a practice which will become very common, the bank will not only have access to all your records but possibly some of your employers' as well. What might be even more threatening, the employer might have access to your private records as well.

Every one of these factors complicates the role of unions and will open further the divide between workers of differing training levels. And every one of them will accentuate the urgency of advanced and continuing education. For many levels, getting a job won't be a problem for those who want one. The real challenge will become income stability and planning for the future (i.e., college education for the children), not employment per se. As already noted, the fastest growing jobs, both as regards numbers and salaries, will all require at least a Bachelors Degree. Those jobs will increase at better than twice the national average and will have the earnings gap augment every year. Skilled workers will simply be more valuable to their employers because they can work more efficiently with more sophisticated tools, and by definition, trained workers can change both tools and assignments much more readily. Those attributes are great employment assets because, as we've seen, the half-life of products, once measured in years, is now often measured in months. As a matter of new market necessity, the next generation of a new product is actually in the tooling stage at the very time the current generation is released to the market. This is a global competitive survival imperative, not a marketing strategy. The diminishing workplace outlook for the untrained is not a matter of politics nor of policy. Neither the leaders nor the locale is material. In the millennium global economy, this condition will be structural and unrelenting. To fail to recognize this key truth is to fail.

Increased corporate competition for skilled people will also decrease the demand for unions and this is another issue to be considered in this setting. Historically, trade union membership has reflected the rise and fall of any industry. The unions have been most aggressively associated with high growth manufacturing and some service industries. To make a well known illustration of the latter category, the size of government increased steadily from 1950 to 1998 and, after the passage of the Civil Service Reform Act of 1978, trade union membership increased sharply among government workers. During the same period American product industries were showing a decline, with industrial union membership degenerating from 35 to 10%.

Even so [3] unionized industries will, in the future, still produce higher salary and fringe benefits for their membership and this factor should certainly be a consideration in career selection. Union shop employees earn about a third higher than non-union employees in the same industries, and discrepancy is even higher, relatively speaking, for minorities and women workers. But, as technology raises professional job numbers, the level of unionization will tend to fall. High demand skills diminish the advantages unions can offer—particularly in the category of job protection. The new information based industries will demonstrate the first experience in union history in which high growth employment will exhibit diminishing union membership in spite of the fact that non-union employees, including professional level, do actually benefit from trade unions.

Lower skill jobs—the types of work traditionally drawing union attention—not only command lower salaries, they are typically the types of jobs most easily automated. [11]For them, job security is a key feature of union membership, surpassing even salary demands. The unions themselves have recognized that attitude. As far back as 1988 an AFL-CIO economist explained national union policy trends toward settling for below inflation wage increases as being mandated by their membership's insistence on job protection over income protection. Competing lower payroll against greater automation would seem to be a very short term, though understandable, strategy because many of those low skilled jobs will inevitably be automated or moved elsewhere. Clearly, union types of occupations will suffer from the simultaneous multiple assaults of job elimination and/or, job export, combined with immigrant competition. Furthermore, "export" doesn't necessarily mean moving to another country. Where once nations competed for industries, now the rivalry is between communities—often neighboring communities. Tax breaks, schools, entertainment facilities, security, and even malls affect corporate move decisions. These are all conditions companies as well as unions cannot control but which nevertheless further limit the benefits and the ability of unions to protect their membership.

The digital conversion actually started in the late 70s but even as recently as the early 90's the balance sheet consequences were negligible. Very few government, industry, or union leaders recognized either the trend or the implications for the working world. The on-the-ground experience of the 80's was further impoverishment of the poor while the educated middle class incomes were close to stationary. During the 90's the information society took off with great consequence and even greater potential. In the late 90s, for the first time in decades, the lowest 10% of the economy were actually making small gains, but the "Wealth Syndrome" was still operative. The wealthier you were, the wealthier you could expect to become. Wealth, while still dominant (rich always helps), was no longer the exclusive pre-condition for success. Education in the 90's demonstrated the first evidence of oncoming Information Age value.

[2]For the purpose of millennium planning, this can't be overstated. The U.S. Department of Labor records indicate that for workers without a high school diploma, real wages fell from $462 a week in 1979 to $337 in 1998. The same trend obtained for workers with a high school diploma even though they started at a slightly higher level. But for workers with a college degree they rose from $758 to $821 over the same period. Even with some gains for the lowest educated levels, the gap continues to enlarge and the Department of Labor forecasts the gap will widen and deepen as the educated worker continues to make gains, while those without post high school education will actually lose ground because of immigration and automation.

[2]Pay gaps between the trained and the less trained are not the only gaps in the labor market, and we ought to pay some attention to those others. They are all important, but the one between men and women is certainly getting the most consideration these days, and for good reason. Although the gap has actually narrowed considerably over the last twenty years, women, on average, only get about

three quarters the salary men get for the same work. Gender differences get more complicated. For instance younger women are almost on a par with men job for job, but middle aged women earn less than seventy cents on their male colleague's dollar.

Some of those differences are somewhat defended by the types of jobs women apply for and the fact that they don't change jobs as often as men do, but nearly half of those differences are based on residual pay patterns which are at least in part, discriminatory. This explanation shows up in the relative pay advances made by white women and minority women where the increase achieved by white women (16% over the last thirty years) are literally double those attained by minority women in precisely the same occupation. Another comparison which illuminates the condition of women as a "minority" is the interesting development that black men, after all these years, have finally ended up on a par with white women. They earn about 75% of white men on average.

Well, what has all this got to do with the millennium? The rejoinder to that question is the constant decree of the Information Age, the more education, the better the outlook. The shortage of trained talent will be serious and getting more so. Things like gender, and race, and origins simply won't matter if profitability or competitiveness is the corporate stake. After World War II, there were virtually no women doctors, very few black lawyers, and literally no minority engineers of any kind. Today, walking through the corridors of any high skill company makes the UN look like an ancient Ivy League college. In general, the greater the skill and/or the higher the education, the less differential is perceived between genders, races, or even disabilities. So here again, the incentives toward higher education will be very high for all, but even higher, relatively speaking, for the disadvantaged of any description.

With all this demand for education and training, how will the school workers,—teachers, teacher's aides, and school administrators fare in the millennium? We can turn, again, to the Bureau of Labor Statistics for guidance and again the figures are telling. The BLS expects a 14% increase in adult and vocational teachers, a 16% increase in K-12 teachers, a 23% increase in university faculty, and a mind boggling 34% increase in special (read "adult") education teachers. This doesn't even count guidance counselors, sports instructors, teachers' aides, administrators, and so on, and over-all it amounts to almost a million additional teaching jobs over the next ten years most of which will not be government sponsored.

[2]Employment is expected to rise from one hundred and twenty million to one hundred and forty million jobs over that period, over half of which increase

will require post high school training. At a target rate of twenty students per additional instructor, all the additional teachers will essentially be taken up by the additional workers' educational requirements. It suggests that a teaching industry which is already strained to capacity limits will be unable to cope with the training update needs which already existed and the shortfall is a concern repeatedly verbalized by the burgeoning information industry. More and more corporations are responding to this very real threat by instituting company sponsored training schools and programs. The effort will clearly be forced to grow. More than likely the results will still be inadequate in terms of sheer numbers and since market systems traditionally attempt to fill market demands, private initiatives will also attempt to fill the void. There will be some great innovative efforts like computer based systems and Internet based courses and probably others not yet on the books.

However that need is ultimately satisfied, it is abundantly clear, to repeat, education, like health, is going to be a very strong growth industry. With this kind of expectation, it would seem indicated that teaching might not be a get-rich plan but it will be a good career choice in general, and an excellent pick for minorities. As another incentive, like medical work, teaching jobs will tend to be long term and stable. Also like the medical sector, the education industry will undergo many basic structural changes because it is not merely the sheer number of students driving the alterations and that will equate to new opportunities. At this point in time, most of the students who constitute the "customer" base for training institutions are still non-voting, non-tax paying children who have little voice in the location and the quality of their schools or, for that matter, of their teachers. As voting adults with an immediate stake in the results of update training, enter the education system, the situation will be transformed. Taxes, politicians, and unions will be forced to accommodate a very demanding customer on issues considerably more concrete than most political differences. Teaching will become a growth industry with teachers themselves becoming better paid, and more respected, but probably, like all the other service industries of the Information Age, less protected.

Summary:

The most fundamental fact of the millennial period is that jobs are moving away from producing "things" to producing information simply because information is more profitable. America might continue to lead the world in the creation, and even the manufacture of merchandise but the expected output increases will be due to productivity improvements rather than plant expansion. Employment growth will be very limited or negative in most production jobs, farms and mining being particular examples. Continuing plant divestiture and consolidations are expected to actually shrink plant size and process. This prediction will probably be more compelling for large capitalization corporations than of their smaller counterparts. Outsourcing encourages new product development at a time of accelerating product evolution. Subcontracting will become a dominating factor of workplace life which means job skills and job locations will become nomadic which in turn means unions will need to dramatically revise their operating strategies if they are to survive and remain effective.

For the American workplace, this is a root transformation of perspective from a very long labor history. The service sector is going to be the dominating area of national growth and personal opportunity. By the end of the first decade of this century they are expected to account for three out of every four jobs in America. But even within the high growth category, some jobs will have more future than others. [3]The much publicized elimination of paper work which was forecast for the computer has, in fact, not yet materialized, but electronic word processing, for example, will be a prerequisite skill. However, by itself, word processing will not be a job with a future.

And finally, there are three basic features of the information age with specific regard to the workplace. The first is that it is functionally irreversible. It is now as much a part of the new industrial America as the smokestack was of the old. The second is that the high tech changes are reaching every manner of making a living. Even McDonald's uses computerized order taking and customer billing. For this reason, education has emerged from being a personal option to being a national priority. Both major parties have acknowledged this expectation and their only difference is "how" not "whether".

[3]And the third, perhaps most notable, the modal shift from products to information will open more economic prospects for more people. As always, there is a penalty. For the nation the price is increased investment in education for all of its citizens. For the worker the consequence is investing his time and energy in continuing education and the increased probability of job change. Many of the old jobs will remain (McDonald's might always need janitors). But for those who understand the new rules, the payback is likely to be realized in higher lifetime earnings. The information age will breach many age old restrictions such as class, age, gender, ethnicity, race, disabilities, and all the other factors of the "glass ceiling". In prior times, family and money were the keys to

success. In the new age brains and education will be added to the mix. A lot more people have brains than have money.

That's real democracy on a working level.

Reading and Reference:

[1] *Futurework*-U.S. Dept. of Labor]

[2] *BLS Looks Ahead to 2008]*

[3] *The 1998-2008 Job Outlook in Brief. BLS]*

[4] *Cheating Death*, Cetron & Owens 0 312 18065 9

[5] *Megatrends* John Nailbitt 0 446 51251

[6] *Boiling Point, the Decline of Middle Class Prosperity* Kevin Phillips 0 679 40461 9

[7] *The End of Work* Jeremy Rifkin0 87477 824 7

[8] *Probable Tomorrows* Cetron and Davies 0 312 15429 1

[9] *Post-Capitalist Society* Peter Drucker 0 88730 661 6

[10] *The Third Wave* Alvin Toffler 0 76783 00799

[11] *Labor and the National Economy* Bowen and Ashenfelter 0 393 09996 2

[12] *Time Magazine* May 22, 2000

[13] The New York Times Magazine March 5, 2000

7

Retirement—Freedom of Choice

Technology always downloads bewildering changes. The discovery of farming presaged the end of the hunter-gatherer economy. The invention of money ended the barter system. The printing press ended church hegemony. Every one of the great waves of discovery originated for narrow purpose and changed the human world. (As a matter of interest, it is very small overstatement to recognize that most great science started as blasphemy. Mortality itself is the next ancient axiom being challenged by science.) The two most difficult problems of senior adjustment in the next decades will be conversion from an analog environment to a digital one, and—possibly more difficult—the extension of life span from under a century to over a century. It sounds simple, as from devices operated by knobs to those operated by buttons. In truth, it will soon require digital skills to boil water but more generally, as shopping, entertainment, telephones, automobiles, and most important, their children and grandchildren go digital, older people are going to be living in a world getting more alien by the day. [3]Being graduates of the past era, retirees have seen so much history being made that they are probably the most adaptable older people ever but a social conversion of this magnitude and rapidity has never been experienced before. That aspect of their world won't be easy but there will be additional problems...and some very real benefits.

Almost any activity is conventionally age related. Products are targeted at age groups. Laws and practice—the draft, the vote, driving, drinking, even theater tickets, are written around age categories. Retirement, in particular, is determined by chronology and almost characteristically associated with "incapacity". In ancient Greece, the average life span was twenty two years, though in that same Greece, Sophocles lived to age ninety and fathered children in his seventies. Nearly two thousand years later, the nineteenth century German Count von Bismarck set up what is now referred to as "Social Security" ostensibly to support workers in their retirement after age sixty five. In point of fact, less than one in twenty workers of the time ever reached that age so this policy was more politics than policy. In 1935, the United States duplicated Bismarck's program, and for the same threshold age. The conceptual difference was that in the 1930's the average age of death was about seventy five so that more than half of the recipients did, in fact, survive to collect at least a few years of the benefit. In 1938 there were less than two million recipients. [12]By 1990 there were thirty one million retirees. Ten years later, there were 35 million and by 2040 it is anticipated that there will be in excess of 75 million retired people in America. In the year 1960, the worker-to-retiree ratio was at least 8 to 1, i.e., eight workers were supporting one retiree. Now it is more like 2 to 1 going toward less than one to one. And that is without any dramatic life extension.

[3][4][5] But people are going to live longer—much longer. Amazingly, the computer models indicate that the aging population will not only *be* healthier, they will *remain* healthier for longer than is now the case. There are already emerging clues suggesting this outcome. Based on the rates of 1982, there should have been over 8 million seriously disabled retired people in 1996. In fact, there were "only" around 7 million. The difference is technology. That Methuselah effort has been so hugely successful that American life expectancy almost doubled.

[7]The modern health industry thrust is *not* directed at control or cures. The new goal is the eradication of illness up to and *including death itself*. However, think about the peripheral effects. Consider what will happen if, for instance, new age medicine extends life expectance from seventy five to one hundred. (The actual goal is one hundred and twenty.) The first consequence is that the majority of the population will be retired and supported by a much smaller number of workers. The age of retirement will clearly need to be advanced, say to eighty for fiscal reasons if none other. [4]That will delay the rotation of jobs from older to younger workers. Since the same technology is upgrading the knowledge prerequisites for job eligibility, many older people might start taking entry level jobs now being filled by young people. [3][[5]Grand parents might be competing for jobs with their grand children. School years will need to be extended far beyond their current grade. Schools will need to be established for groups currently sidelined because of their age. Modern smart machinery is far more efficient and produces more output with fewer work hours. In order to maintain the living standards of those still working, productivity would need to increase faster than the retiree/worker ratio. That would reduce the number of jobs. Innovation will need, therefore, to produce added markets at a rate faster than the vanishing old markets would reduce the number of jobs.

The World War II generation had the depression inspired Social Security program and the post war rise in real estate values. They had the relatively long post war economic booms that produced the Medicare program and an assortment of pension plans. The relative net income security of those years as well as the income insecurity of previous years encouraged savings. That combination has already vanished as an operational circumstance for the next generation and the anticipated extension of life will actually intensify the quandary. As an illustration, most pension programs have a minimum service requirement such as full year of employment. In high turnover industries, the companies will change the minimum service requirement to whatever they deem necessary to keep only necessary employees. Most employees will then have to finance their own pension fund out of their own salaries, a withdrawal that could easily reach 25% of after-tax income if the life span expectation is increased. Furthermore, the frequent job turnover that will be almost typical in the next decades is not without cost. It often involves moving families, which might affect dual incomes, as well as retraining expenses, both of which would affect savings. If life span lengthens significantly, most retirees will run out of life savings long before they run out of life span. They are obviously more prone to lose their life's companion for longer periods of time because longer life is likely to extend differences in mortality. [12]To make this scene still darker, both Social Security and Medicare are both already in trouble and are sure to be modified even without life span extension. In fact, if longer, healthier life becomes a reality, Social Security might be forced to reverse course and become an aid program for the disabled. That might turn out to be a plus because at that point the tradition of multi generational households might actually reappear. Conversely, that total context would negatively affect marriage stability, children's education, church affiliations, and even political identity.

Choosing to retain a retirement age set over a century before has had some unexpected and certainly many unintended, consequences. Where previously workers had essentially worked until they were incapacitated or dead, now they could retire to be replaced with younger workers. In the future, that is going to be an important factor for the country to consider. If, as a nation we will live longer, we will probably work later than at any time in history. Later retirement will affect jobs from entry level to advancement.

Longer life span traditionally implied more time in nursing homes or an assisted living facility. "Assisted living" homes are residences in which older people who are still essentially functionally independent are able to come and go, as well as live as they choose. The resident uses what he needs and the facility changes its level of assistance as new supports are needed. And here too, modern technology is going to make a great difference, from smart equipment that reduces the required qualifications of nursing home attendants, to emergency equipment that allows crisis treatment and on to sophisticated communications for summoning quick help. Homes are already being designed with video and audio monitors in each room so that elderly people living alone are actually never quite alone. They will be wired or networked into caretaker monitors, senior citizens community centers, or medical facilities. For those at greater risk, dual function equipment is becoming available that will turn a monitor on or produce an instant alarm at the appropriate center. One such device is a pacemaker which sounds a "911" alarm when it detects an *oncoming* emergency. Another is a defibrillator that accomplishes programmed analysis and acts instantly to correct heartbeat. Touch screens are now being produced that allow either able bodied or disabled people to receive or send information with a simple touch to pre-selected screen locations. Motion sensors, heat sensors, as well as special sound sensors are already extant that transmit automatic information. Sounds futuristic? Nothing of the kind! Every one of these items are already available at specialty outlets with relatively low and dropping prices—far lower than any assisted living facility costs. This kind of technology will allow seniors to remain in the own homes far longer than is now imagined. Test polls already taken indicate that most seniors have a clear sense of gained independence and involvement. As a very large and growing population, older people will be more stationary, with more to offer the rest of the community than ever before. Senior citizens will be more active and have more group options. Indeed, they will be less "senior" and more intolerant of any form of disrespect that was characteristic of the prior times.

[1][4][5]Financial security is a major source for the waters of the "Fountain of Youth". Adventurousness incites a desire to learn, and to travel, and to experience what the retired state allows. But for all, rich and poor alike, new activities and benefits are appearing so fast that they are, in fact, somewhat bewildering. New technologies are encouraging new lifestyles. To begin with, "retirement" no longer necessarily signifies the end of employment. With ever increasing frequency and life span, it will mean a "career change" from the necessities of making a living to the desire to make a life. Expertise may change with time, but judgment, otherwise known as "wisdom", is cumulative. In this age of specialization, retirees are becoming a dynamic reference in virtually every industry because depth is notably missing in a workplace where novelty is a dominating factor.

[3] Senior salesmen who sold out of out of their briefcase by necessity will sell out of their home for efficiency. Retirees are visible everywhere from bagging gro-

ceries to teaching public schools and universities. Retired engineers with musical talents are showing up in new orchestras and putting on an astonishingly good performance. Teachers are retiring to write that long suppressed novel. Foreign language instructors are appearing in international corporations and even the CIA. In this age of almost unlimited access to knowledge, experienced judgment gives reference judgment a pretty good race and insight is usually the exclusive product of maturity. Instinct will always be an important asset, and seniors are just as likely to have it. (For very ancient reasons, most societies are convinced that being "old" is analogous with being smart".)

As usual in this age, the higher your education or skill level, the more likely it is that you will find a niche, as an employee, an entrepreneur, or a consultant. Seniors have some real advantages for the right situation. Many don't need most of the fringes, including medical insurance. They probably don't actually want a full time job so they get paid when they want to work. And on top of all of that, in this era of rapid product maturity, most companies have obsolete process and products which are still lucrative enough to produce but not profitable enough to train new personnel. Hiring a part timer for such operations is a great deal more practical than a full time employee and more and more companies learning the lesson that mature employees of that category are very reliable, not withstanding their chronological age. Despite Federal discrimination statutes, many healthy employees are induced to retire as a matter of impersonal corporate policy rather than the employee's residual capability. With the escalating roll of entrepreneurship in this age of rapid market changes, low payroll is not only important for operating, it's vital for start-ups. Hiring retired, experienced people who don't need fringes and who aren't interested in moving around will be a real multiple benefit for small companies—the same ones that will be responsible for most of the job growth—and only retirees offer that facility. Some companies are still in the process of learning that lesson and are not quite ready to step away from the past. As a general rule retirees are looking to enhance income, stay useful or at least occupied, and even enjoy themselves while they are at it. They are most specifically not looking for careers but, as a matter of fact, the Federal Age Discrimination in Employment Act makes it illegal to discriminate against people in the age range of forty to seventy years. With the general population growing older but staying healthier and more alert, that mind-set, and the law as well, will obviously change.

It may not only be an obsolete bias of corporate America which restricts opportunities for senior citizens, but rather the citizens themselves. The twentieth century was, in its' own way, probably the most extraordinary period of the last millennium and many of its alumnae's lives reflect that dynamism. Those who recognize their own vitality beyond the aging syndrome will encounter opportunities in their "second lives" that they may never have had in their first. There will, of course, still be recessions but the trend line for all employment over high technology periods is upward, and for high tech skills, is dramatically upward—so much so that, as already noted, most skill based corporations are actually predicting long term talent shortages in spite of periodic recessions. With any proficiency and any retirement income, such as Social Security, trained retirees will probably have more personal options rather than less.

[3][5]That's only one of many reasons why senior education courses are on the upswing. More colleges every year are introducing professional level courses specifically structured for retirees and many states are recognizing the asset value of retirees and providing this education at highly discounted prices, sometimes, as in Georgia, actually free. You provide your own books and transportation and the state provides the instruction. As a matter of record, not being limited to professional training any more, retirees are taking courses that interest them. It's the chance most of them didn't have as under-graduates and many are smart enough not to pass it by. For the same reason, New Age senior centers and churches will be hard to recognize. They already provide an astonishing new range of activities that extend far beyond so called "Golden Age Clubs" card playing. Personal computers, VCRs. DVD's, the Internet, cellular phones, and even that dinosaur, radio, permit a level of ongoing engagement that they didn't have as part of the workaday population.

Those new technologies will all encourage a range of learning that begins to compete with the universities. Already available courses include languages, politics, theater, literature, and very practical material such as medical information, legal aid, personal finances, travel and so on. The opportunities for learning will, in the future, be far more varied both as to location and modality. Local churches, public schools, as well as private schools, will use all the technology in their mix. Education for retirees will far exceed the need to know. It will encompass the desire to understand, often missing in some previous "learn by rote" training. In a typical undergraduate course, the student is hopefully challenged. In a retiree course, it will more likely be the instructor who feels challenged. Wisdom is more directly linked to the lacerations of life than the lessons of the classroom and wisdom is what the senior student brings to his course at the first session. Even his choice of subject matter will be more selective because he is aware of fading physical resources, but his interests will more likely expand far beyond those of his prior life, as will his freedom of choice.

Restaurants, theaters, stores, airlines, travel agencies, and universities all have senior discounts and most will have computer ordering access. Even towns have senior tax allowances. (Travel has so many discounts for the senior that roaming has been increasing at the rate of five percent a year for decades. The advent of the single European currency will not only simplify currency exchange, it will reduce the cost. As Internet and video brochures proliferate, destinations, costs, and background information will become available in your kitchen. (The travel industry is long term bullish in spite of the millennial recession and international terrorists, so it is predicted that within the next decade, more than ten percent of American workers will be employed in the hospitality industry.) Even health services, a previously serious retiree problem, will significantly decline as a travel consideration. Medical service, which required specialist and patient to be at the same location, will be delivered without the participants even being on the same continent.

[2][6]Oddly enough, choice is also appropriate to one other empowerment of new age technology. It will allow satisfying solitude. Some have suggested that the most widespread ailment of the aged was isolation. Before retirement, family, jobs, social schedules, responsibilities, all combined to make solitude a luxury. After retirement solitude was finally achievable, but it was at the price of loneliness. That cost was often paid in the coin of depression and illness, the most pronounced symptom of which is the "do-nothing" pattern. "Loneliness" is a pretty indistinct description of a broad array of feeling but at the very least, the range must include loss of relationships. Subsequent to the fellowship of daily commerce, the sudden cut-off of occupation contributes to feelings of worthlessness and exclusion from accustomed colleagues and activities. Some have suggested that a significant contributor to the high cost of Medicare is indeed the need for connectivity, even if that liaison is one's doctor. But connection is a central theme of the new age. Anyone can find peers and links relatively quickly and at little or no cost. Studies in both Britain and the United States show that retirement friendships become a very important component of every other relationship they have. Children live at another location and grand-children usually live on another planet. Distance no longer need mandate disconnect. Rather it will mean options for private time with the touch of a button. Even travel can be researched and arranged with a "click" of that same button. Seclusion will be less a "situation" and more of a selection. Physical limitations will be much less restrictive with the entire world literally at one's fingertips. Compatible groups, formerly difficult to find, and even childhood friends separated for years, become available for catch up and reconnection. Old friends change over the years and the rela-

tionship may not be as compatible at the retirement stage of life as they were in prior stages but the new communications systems permit a level of "test" which allows needy people to sample the relationship without buying them.

The circumstance of "singleness", however arrived at, will never be particularly happy, but need not be the blight of seniority that it once was, for the very same reasons. The connectivity provided by digital television and computers, on to cellular phones, PDA's—Personal Digital Assistants, Palm Pilots, or more probably, some combination of them which combined voice recognition, will permit engagement—including video (live pictures) with kindred souls and kindred needs at the touch of a finger. Finding a friend, a companion, a partner, or even a "chat group" will be more comfortable and far less encumbered by inconveniences like distance and disabilities. Indeed, as accustomed physical interaction diminishes, that relative connection freedom will inevitably lead to associations which are less age defined and more interest specific. That is a very important variation from the experience where residents of senior communities could reasonably conclude that the entire world was ageing. Both adversity and happiness will be more easily shared. Families, half a world apart, will be back in contact. Even finances will be relegated a less significant role.

Women in particular will have many advantages in their retirement during these new times. Their self-image had, at least in part, to do with their marital state and their husband's occupation, while for men, it was largely financial assets. Many would concede that women, like men, become more interesting with age, but few would say more confident with time. On the other hand, between Social Security, pensions, investments, savings, etc., many men are more psychologically secure as retirees than they were in the workforce—and more poised. That divergence will likely almost disappear. As already noted, women will be working in numbers as large as men, their earnings gap will narrow, their savings and investment levels will equalize, and most important, their self esteem will rise as their social status becomes independent of men. The ability to "sample" relationships via technological means will further enhance retired women's willingness to take unaccustomed social excursions. They might lose their "protection" but they will gain their sovereignty. In still another aspect of modern technology, medicine is extending life span of both genders, as well as equalizing that life span between them. Historical data indicates that women over the age of seventy five outnumbered men by as much as two to one. They were far more likely to live alone, with a lower income and a reduced "authority" position even within their own families. Women have almost routinely anticipated elongated widowhood and dependence on their children, to the extent that most life insurance policies were on the lives of their husbands. So the life extension of men and the increasing financial security of women will lighten some of the emotional burdens of children and of husbands as well.

Crime is often the unspoken issue of the retired, a concern which substantially alters their plans and their lifestyles. For this aspect, technology will be both friend and enemy. Crime is usually related to the national economy and for many that long term economy will be better than ever before, as a direct outcome of new technologies. An information age should at the very least, moderate the depths and perhaps the length of cycles while expanding opportunities for more people during upturns. In addition, in another of those "unexpected consequences", millennial terrorism will almost unavoidable improve both national and international police operation and cooperation. Increased surveillance, unwelcome but inevitable in an atmosphere of civilian terrorism, will inadvertently produce a side product of increased personal security. Where human policemen are not available, electronic policing will, perhaps unfortunately, become extremely available. Most of the very sophisticated technologies, originally developed for military purpose, have or will become commercially available for civilian purpose and medical emergency as well.

Even blessings will become worrisome. As life extension becomes more probable, savings accounts and banks, once regarded as the second church of the elderly, will become inadequate investments. In fact, familiar brick and mortar bank tellers will largely be replaced by impersonal ATM's and eventually by PC's. The comfortable feel of United States cash, the "coin of the realm" and indeed the coin of the world, will morph into electronic money usually underwritten by those same banks which became such poor investments. Even worse, electronic money itself will evolve in such myriad forms—bankcards, credit cards, Smart Cards, debit cards, ID cards, etc., that wallets will be designed around credit cards with no accommodation for pictures of grandchildren. As if all that isn't enough, it seems to many elderly citizens that most of the cards carried in a standard wallet—ID's, personal medical information and bank data, driver's licenses, insurance identification, will be another emotional threat if they are collectively replaced by a few mysterious electronic cards which can be lost, (a common phenomenon for seniors) or read without authorization. It's called "identity theft". Even the notion of a Smart Card "pre-loaded with cash" for every day transactions like subway fares or that senior ritual, a cup of coffee with a friend, seems at the very least, bizarre. For survivors of earlier times all of that translates to one's entire life being exposed on unfamiliar, probably unchecked and definitely unreadable credit cards which seem easy to misuse. Where once retiree safety concerns was dominated by physical predation, the very technologies which will open new vistas to them will also expose them to new forms of financial assault that most don't understand and which are literally innovating every day. The notion of "identity theft" is alien to any self-concept they ever had. That is all a very unnerving but highly probable millennial vision.

In the multi-ethnic world of tomorrow, enclaves, like bias, will be much more difficult to preserve. Racial relations are still far from ideal but few would deny the improvement. With time, opportunity, and technology related motivation, that relic of the past will substantially diminish. Seniors mostly don't have that time and for them accustomed attitudes don't change without energy input—usually on short supply. However, in spite of appearances, the advent of ethnic adult communities is not necessarily ascribable to prejudice. For seniors, everything familiar in their lives is frighteningly slipping away. Recognizable foods, clothes, shops, cultures, religions, and faces, are an almost desperate effort to slow the visible passage of time. The financial gap between retired racial and financial groups is only a further irritant to this progression as it is even between former home owners and renters. But here again the applied science of the new inclusive planet will offer at least some relief. Ever more cable channels are now broadcasting foreign language programs. Consumer Internet equipment is coming out at lower and lower prices that do not require much more than elemental literacy levels. Churches and community centers are well into acquiring basic computer equipment which allows their members to stay connected and to find family and compadre's of compatible mind. More churches every day are now sponsoring psychological "support courses" and genealogy programs specifically organized to adjust senior citizens to the outside new world as well as their personal new world.

As a very identifiable segment, on the whole, seniors will have more recognition, and more available facility than at any time in history. This will be their time.

Summary:

The obsession has always been on "youth" and understandably so. That's where the money was. In this century, technology will append a major new adjunct to each of the traditional lower, middle, and upper classes—namely the retirees. That class is already over twenty percent of any vote and will probably develop even more political clout than any of the others simply because they will be more conscious of their interests as a cross class group, many will have more money to donate to their causes, and all will have more time to be political. Many of their age related narrow interests override more broad concerns of religion, race, origin, culture and other individual attitudes that separate people—perhaps the only consortium of such otherwise diverse character. The American Association of Retired Persons (AARP) was founded in 1958 originally to provide insurance for the elderly. The AARP is the largest special interest group in the United States and growing fast. With a membership now larger than the populations of most nations, its publication, "Maturity" has the third largest circulation in the country. The organization also distributes voter's guides with far too much influence for politicians to ignore.

AARP is not alone. There is the National Committee to Preserve Social Security, the National Council of Senior Citizens, literally tens of thousands of local church senior "clubs", and senior community centers, to mention only several. As a political group they vote at substantially higher rates than do younger voters. Adding to seniors, and often voting in sympathy, both women and immigrants, as voting constituencies, are growing faster than most other groups and both of them will age. For them, subjects like the economy and the environment are important, but less compelling than healthcare, which is literally a life and death issue for many of them. Senior organizations usually don't necessarily support particular party candidates, but they usually have a clear understanding of their own self interest as senior citizens which is not as typical for most other wide spectrum groups.

Yet, in spite of the growing political weight of current and potential senior citizens, there is one concern of "soon to be seniors" that will ultimately outweigh them and that is the budget. As life spans increase markedly and the national cost of supporting non-producing citizens rises without apparent limits, some kind of restrictions will clearly become mandatory and the most obvious, the most expensive, the most expansive program—Social Security—will inevitably be reviewed in many critical aspects as regards age of retirement, income of the retiree, extent of benefits, and inflation indexing. The most often mentioned changes are means testing and benefit taxing. Even with these changes, it is very likely that science will extend life faster than politics will extend funding. At some point in the next two generations, budgetary realities will inescapably compel a very painful revisit to this political third rail.

Along with Social Security, medical benefits rank high on retirees list of priorities. Those benefits are not counted as income but are expanding every year since the inception of the program in the '60s. Over one third of the moneys spent on health care is spent by the seniors who represent (at the moment) only twenty percent of the American population. Medicare, at this point, will pay for some pharmacy but no dental although organizations like AARP have so much market clout that they are able to get pharmacy discounts for their membership and they offer dental insurance for a price.

Under present day political conditions, there are few incentives aside from financial, for limiting medical procedures and many incentives, very understandably, to expand them. Medical technology is expanding so rapidly, both as to methodology and availability, that newly permitted procedures are a very common event. During the immediate period of the new century, there is very little doubt than some level of pharmacy will be added to the Medicare mandate. Not long afterward, it would seem likely that dental will be added and ultimately nursing home care will be demanded. Suffices to say, the new period is going to see some very high national medical services bills and some very deep national soul searching Will the elderly develop disproportionate political clout? Will Marx's economic warfare projection be replaced by age warfare? Are the young being taxed to support the old? Are limited medical facilities being diverted from the young with a future to the seniors without one? Still, they will live longer, becoming a much larger part of the population and vote in greater numbers. In the millennium, the traditional picture of "old" is going to undergo some very profound changes along with the notion of being "put out to pasture".

In a more general category, growth of the senior population might have some salutary influence on the nation. There will still be class differences but within the classes, seniors will have more issues in common than divisions. Certainly, within those economic classes there will be much more cultural and racial diversity than was the case in the past. By and large they will tend to watch the same information programs and motion pictures. More and more will become active participants on the Internet. Senior oriented school classes will bring them into broader contact as adults than they had previously experienced as children. With more leisure time over a longer life spans and dispersed families, they will travel more often and that too will tend to reduce "local" bias particularly as everyone becomes part of a minority. Furthermore, the world wide reach of the Internet is already attracting many seniors to the computer because of the ease of e-mail communications. To some extent influenced by the senior market, e-mail equipment is being simplified with new products showing up that don't even require a computer or a cell phone and actually cost less. Such equipment is about the size of (and in fact included in) a cell phone and fits in the pocket so that people can stay in touch on a twenty four hour basis almost regardless of location in the entire world. That not only makes travel a bit less intimidating, it actually allows "home" to come along. Those same products sell to smaller but growing markets such as immigrant populations.

Summing it all up, "retiring" in the twenty-first century will be a very different experience than it was in the previous century. The most important difference is the dramatic extension of life span that implies that the mean age of the retiree group will be much greater than it had been and that their average health will be much improved. That means retirees will be much more active physically, socially, and politically. It means that merely "baby sitting" grandparents will be neither sufficient nor satisfactory. The age shift will modify the school house, the work place, the entertainment industry, the medical business, the social structure, and perhaps, even the religious organizations. Seniors in this century will have more personal options than any prior generation. At the same time, the longevity may itself become a threat if they outlive their financial resources.

Be all that as it may, the profound underlying reality of the millennial age is that there never was a better time to be retired.

Reading and Reference:

[1] *The Senior Citizen Handbook* Stokell & Kennedy 0 13 806514 4

[2] *Leisure—Time for Living and Retirement* Margaret E. Mulac

[3] *Second Wind* Philip J. Kelly

[4] *Future Work* James Robertson

[5] *Ageing in Modern Society* Dorothy Jerrome

[6] *The Elderly, Opposing Viewpoints* Bender & Leone 0 89908 450 8

[7] *Cheating Death* Cetron & Davies 0 312 18065 9

[8] AJC Sunday, March 10,2002 P-Q1

[9] *The Essential Guide to Digital Set-top Boxes & Interactive TV* G.O'Driscoll 0 13 017360 6

[10] *The Economist* December 14, 2002

[11] *IEEE Spectrum* Technology Survey 2003

8

Entertainment—The Perpetual Domain

Choice is a driving concept of the time and nowhere more evident than in entertainment—preference as to media, format, time, language, even preference as to subtitles. The Internet will make much more than mere entertainment available. Banking, shopping, business, personal contacts are all coming "on-line. Chat groups, the library, books, music are already on-line. And the receiver might be an audio system, a pocket "radio", a full projections screen, or a hand held screen. The program might originate as a live broadcast, an analog recording, or more likely, a digital recording, or it might be a computer simulated program. These myriad delivery and receiving personal preferences will turn the entertainment industry on its head in the next decade.

[7]The most commercially widespread application began with music. By means of digital compression, music can be downloaded in minutes rather than hours and transmitted over the Internet. That development, called MP3, transforms the music business because it permits music to be downloaded from the Internet without that trifling detail of paying for it. It would also cause a revolution in copyright law. Content producers find it virtually impossible to protect their subject matter so the industry will be looking for new ways to make content profitable through other means, such as licensing under very ingenious guises. One approach, copied from the early radio experience has the producer selling (or giving) license for unlimited reproduction for non-commercial purpose with conditions, such as sales pitches for other products, other companies, personal profile information for each copy recipient, or whatever gives them a revenue source. (Historically, broadcast radio began to advertise products as the only way to produce an income since there was no practical way to charge for receiving broadcasts) In short, the music itself becomes a sales pitch. With that approach the Internet becomes an earnings source for the creators and the producers instead of

an open door to program hijackers. Even the "licensing" arrangements are subject to many innovations as for instance a monthly membership instead of a per item charge. This is a very new way for an old industry to make a living but it conforms to the model of entertainment on demand.

Entertainment on demand sounds like an escapist's paradise but all the major studios are already setting up libraries in anticipation of commercial equipment which will doubtless be mass marketed within the next three to five years. Music in this mode is already commercially available but motion pictures are a more difficult problem. The dilemma with the motion picture aspect of the concept is stuffing a lot of information through a constricted channel in a short time. Just by way of explanation a typical one and one half hour motion picture would probably contain the equivalent of seven hundred million English words in terms of digital information. Under ordinary circumstances that picture would take many hours to transmit. But this age of novelty is no ordinary era and a number of techniques have already evolved to reduce this problem. The major approach has been a system named "Codec" (Compression-Decompression) which is actually simpler to describe than to accomplish. Basically the idea separates stationary parts of a scene from the action, i.e., the background from the actors. The information conveying the background is then transmitted once during the scene rather than in every frame. This is analogous to modern electronic pianos where the drum beat sound is introduced one time and repeated automatically throughout a melody without the pianist actually doing anything at all. The picture frame is then reassembled at the display. Most of the known software companies (Microsoft, Apple, etc.,) are well into such development, as are many of the lesser and unknown companies.

In anticipation of this new competition, AOL-Time Warner intended their merger to capitalize on the future potential of being one of the first cable video on demand systems that will permit (initially) one way viewing of any stocked library program material including news, sports, motion pictures, games, and financial market activity for starters, but eventually leading to all interactive reception. The viewer will not only choose content, but pauses, forward and rewinds, even camera angles and advertising material.

Consumer choice is going to cause far more drama on both Wall Street and Main Street (not to mention Broadway) than is apparent at first glance. Just for beginners, most film presentation is currently dominated by theater, cable TV, DVD, and VCR tape companies. This advance would return control of that industry to the consumer electronics manufacturers that produced the new CODEC equipment which, conceivably, could handle inputs from any source, including, the Internet. For the Main Street audience, such equipment will rapidly displace the VCR (and even the DVD) which produced most of the sales and profits for the consumer electronics industry. Tape recording ability shaped the entertainment habits of almost all Americans, and a considerable part of the rest of the world. It will create entirely new generations of pocket type wireless devices as yet unconceived with social effects unimagined. The technological problems will sooner or later—and probably sooner—be resolved. In an almost striking repetition of the medical pharmacy industry, the great hurdle will be ownership rights. Each of the current systems includes many techniques protected by out of house patents.

Practically speaking, patent protection for the inventor or the inventor's sponsor is still the only incentive for invention and they are only valuable if they actually reach the market. While protection of patent rights are necessary, the economic reality is that a "per set" royalty for the patent owner will be impractical to assess. Furthermore, a royalty of as little as one cent per show would quickly put any content distributor out of business because there will be millions of "receivers" tuned to the same program. The distributor would be facing the enigma of making less money with more viewers. However, this, also like pharmacy, is another example of market place operating. Nobody gets to make any money unless his product is sold and there is enough competition in this "compression-decompression" technology to almost guarantee its widespread market place appearance in the very near future. This is a situation very similar to the "Microsoft" problem where the very first software developer who can produce an economically viable "user friendly" package is very likely to become a single source with all the content producers jumping on his bandwagon.

The other simile which is worth mentioning reminds one that the computer started as a government census program aid from which it graduated to a universal business necessity. Who could have imagined this piece of equipment becoming so vital to a society that children are being taught to use it? These digital compression-decompression techniques have a latent portent of commercial commotion for a world becoming more digitalized every day.

As a matter of interest, some limited versions of "TV at convenience" are available even now in a type of computerized TV accessory with a built-in hard disc, which can be programmed to automatically record anything you prefer on a hard disc so that you can watch or hear the program at your own leisure. Although this is not "video on demand", you can instruct the computer to record all volley ball games without necessarily knowing whether there are any such events programmed. The difference in the new age is source. As of now, such recording is limited to TV programming which comes in on a cable or dish. The new technology will source from any origin—anything, in fact, that will be available on the Internet, cable, or broadcast. As an interesting aside, compression technology might obsolete the personal computer. This concept places keyboards in the home and the actual computer at the server's facility along with personal data which is now saved on a personal hard disc. Server stored data will be available precisely as it is on today's PCs. As an added advantage, the server would then be responsible for security and virus protection. That would drastically change the commercial basis of the PC industry, cut the prices, sizes, and configuration of home computing equipment, and produce a potentially enormous new service industry which does not even exist at this point. The wave of the future is renting, not owning.

In a parallel direction, in October of 2001, the Microsoft Corporation initiated a new service which permits subscribers to watch everything from current movies to old TV programs on their PC's or on digital TV sets interconnected with their PC. This video on demand system will allow their customers to start, pause, restart, repeat, and fast forward—and digitally record if so desired (although, again, the future of "owning" recordings of any kind seems very dim, at best). There are many hurdles to their program, not the least of which is the requirement for cable modems and very fast equipment processor speeds which most PC owners do not have—as yet. It also assumes that their customers will accept motion pictures shown on PC's when they have DVD's and theater TV systems available.

[4]Program material on demand is anticipated to become a large market with many product input approaches. A real world market limitation would appear to be that very assortment and complexity of equipment intended to handle all this potential sourcing. Not to worry. With a market of such variability it is not surprising that solutions are already in the pipeline in spite of the "in-process" condition of many of the devices. A large number of companies are working on a single package conception with vastly improved operating simplicity. They will combine all the anticipated service functions of the future. The equipment will include program planning features, video and music play, record, printout, playback, archive, photograph display, for AM, FM, Digital, Analog, e-mail, and even distribution to various devices around the house or office. Several companies are also planning to include non-entertainment housekeeping functions such as security, fire, and home equipment monitoring, all in a single console. The equipment will optionally include printers and hard discs that will permit copying from DVD's and CD's as well as accessory inputs like broadcast TV, digital

cameras, cable modems, microphones and phonographs. Apple Computer, one of the hustlers for this device, calls it a "digital hub". The output distribution to home and office accessories will likely be wireless. In line with the nature of the service environment of the coming market, the money is expected to be made in subscriptions for each of the service inputs much as cable companies now charge for "pay per view".

This is very much up to the minute technology. Very well known companies like Motorola, Royal Philips Electronics, Apple Computer, Microsoft, and Pioneer are knee deep in such development programs. Add to that the start-ups like Moxi Digital, Metro Link, Cirrus Logic, and Digeo Inc. and then include the many software writing service companies with whom these afore-mentioned companies are cooperating. Many, perhaps most, of the apparent technical problems of the coming era are more a matter of economics than of technology. The technologies are, in fact being resolved as we speak but they are required by both market and federal considerations to take account of the number of analog TV sets, for example, already out there in much the same manner that oncoming color TV once had to accommodate the huge number of black and white TV's at that time. The introduction of digital TV, with its many proven advantages, is experiencing the same combination market and legal constraints. Quite aside from the economics of replacing millions of analog TV sets, and the huge number of accessory attachments associated with them, there is even the more basic problem of customer adaptation to a whole new set of operating procedures and terms—perhaps easy for some but not for the majority.

As a simple example, digital TV will make available many more channels and many brand new services (probably including voting) with accessory "set-top" boxes, but set owners will need to know how to navigate their set programs to use this new resource. There are new on-screen applications being developed to accomplish this navigation purpose—as for instance to find TV programs. One particular system is called EPG (Electronic Program Guides) through which customers will be able to browse by program titles, subjects, times, dates, and many other key words. The consumer will still need to acquire a working knowledge of how to operate this equipment and EPG will include "how-to" programming for the dizzying array of new digital television possibilities such as interactive channel browsing, on-line banking, and shopping. Digital television in combination with EPG type software will also enable additional services such as program alerts, favorite program selections, and program subject matter searches. Add to all of that the oncoming programmed home education hours. The biggest hurdle might be setting all these new "how-to" menus in English rather than the gibberish common to most current help versions.

It goes without saying that all this newly available (and accessible) programming is going to cause real concerns for parents who want to control both the quantity and the quality of what their children are viewing. It is very likely that the existence of hundreds of channels, many of them changing content as fast as they change ownership, and hundreds of available hours is going to overwhelm "the parent chip" with the result that parents are going to have to take more direct charge of what and how much their children watch either with a lock (not very likely) or with a PIN number (much more likely) but again in this age of personal choices, personal responsibility will need to play a larger role. It also goes without saying that literacy, and in particular, digital literacy, will experience widespread learning motivation and will absolutely inescapably become a fundamental educational requirement…as well as asset.

Regardless of the specifics of these particular ventures, their launch demonstrates the direction that digital entertainment, indeed the digital world, is going and the extent to which it will likely produce an "at your convenience" audience in an era where time and convenience will become a key factor in the audience market. As has already been noted, all of this is generating enormous headaches regarding intellectual property rights. Written materials such as books and articles, motion pictures and music are usually copyrighted. The copyright, like patent protection, is how creative people get paid. At one time patents were considered to be more valuable than copyrights. Today's technology is moving so rapidly that inventions may be outmoded by the time the patent is actually issued which leaves many corporations with serious questions about the value of patent efforts unless they already have follow-on technologies. On the other hand, intellectual material such as art and literature might have less instant value but also have better "shelf life". Mozart and Shakespeare have more total audience in a single TV broadcast of today than they had during their entire lifetimes, so that technology challenges to copyrights have serious business implications. As more and more copyrighted material gets on the Internet, the software and hardware for replication will become more and more commonly available from personal computers. Digital copies are as good, and sometimes can be doctored to be even better than the originating version. Aside from the possibility that the reproduction capability might cut out tens of thousands of CD and DVD distributor jobs, it could mortally damage the creative rights of ownership. This technology even has international implications. How, for example, will the United States challenge China's black market CD producers if thirty or forty million American homes can commit precisely the same act with impunity? This has been compared to producing cars with universal ignition keys.

High quality reproduction equipment is so certain to appear in the near term that legislation is now being programmed for congressional hearing that would require producers to install automatic limiting circuitry which would prevent replication of copyrighted material but PC producers claim that the ability to produce "print-outs" is fundamental to PC sales and that it would inhibit legitimate business activities. They make the analogy of being able to copy music from radio programs or make VCR copies of TV programs. They point out that more than half of the PC's now sold include CD-writable drives (called "burners") with the percentage going up every year. Gateway even has a music download area on its Website. Apple computer is actively encouraging the private production of CD's with its campaign of "Rip, Mix, and Burn". PC based companies like Dell, Intel, Cisco and even IBM are claiming that legal restrictions would damage the American leadership of the PC industry, and possibly mortally wound the American chip industry. That is a not too subtle form of blackmail because the United States is now a world leader of "smart applications" which is generating almost all of the science this volume mentions. The chip industry also insists that legislation now pending before congress would prevent people from copying CDs that they already own. On the other hand, the Recording Industry Association of America (RIAA) demands that equipment producers include technology which prevents the illegal recording of copyrighted material merely to protect "intellectual material" laws which are already on the books. Therein lays the rub. If copyrights are protected from marketable technologies, why not patents? If neither is protected, what will motivate innovation? The difficult quandary is basically moral because it has already been judged as illegal. This battle is one of the first of the new era cultural conflicts driven by technology that is very unique to that era. Entertainment (and industry) equipment capability is growing so fast that it is difficult for standards—legal as well as technical—to keep pace. Culture always lags science. (Or, as some scientists assert, "science always drags culture".) Nevertheless, challenges are appearing and will continue to emerge. Of course, the real shocker will appear if and when PCs themselves are made obsolete by the identical technological development. There is much more to come on this subject.

Those battles will be fought in the courts of the twenty-first century, rather than the development labs. There will be one hurdle more difficult yet than even the legalities and that is the market. Very much like the black and white television of the mid twentieth century, it will take time for customers to replace so much unrelated and unsupported existing equipment with universal consoles.

That time gap actually leaves an opening for some service or facility not yet envisioned, to fill the function of an enticement to such a serious conversion. Still, in this radically creative period, it would almost be remarkable if some such knight in shining armor did not appear.

The gist of this discussion applies directly to entertainment applications, but like all technologies, there will be indirect implications for related purposes. As an example, a good deal of what we Americans consider "free" entertainment is, of course, subsidized by advertising. Without it, radio, the Internet, television, and even cable vision would be considerably less available. While even the most fervent "protectionists" agree that Internet is by far the most effective means of getting creative intellectual material out, no viable business model has yet surfaced to allow artists and writers to make a living. Not only does modern entertainment equipment permit selective screening of advertisements but Internet and wireless devices will further erode the audiences of older technologies from which they do earn a return. At the same time, all of this new "on demand" technology permits vendors to track consumer patterns. Vendors can associate buying patterns with subscription habits to produce "models" for each family, including family size, gender distribution, ethnic patterns, and economic class. In aggregate, the models will facilitate "guided" electronic sales pitches. Such equipment opens channels of advertising which were never before available and subtracts advertising funds from the conventional conduits of entertainment. And it is not just entertainment which will feel the impact. Newspapers and magazines as well, depend on advertising to maintain profitability and they too will see reduced revenues due to the new technologies.

[6]"News", until recently, was not even considered to be entertainment so it is very interesting to realize that many of the same technological changes are making the news as available as entertainment with great implication. With all these sources, the so called "talking heads" i.e., "experts", will lose audience as well as sponsorship. That will change the current events network functions and there are some international considerations evolving unexpectedly. As an example, the United States has, since the Unesco Conference of 1945, been pressing for the free flow of information. While the argument has been based on the idea of "open societies", the reality has resulted in the one way flow of information, mostly originating in the west, and the United States in particular. The third world has, in effect, become "information dependencies" of the United States. American technology almost mandates American domination of what is transmitted by satellites. Since the news is largely paid for by commercials, it also permits American domination of international advertising. Modern Internet

technology will change that landscape. For the first time in a very long time, foreign firms will not only have reasonably fair access to international advertising but interactivity will permit on the spot challenges to event interpretation such as has never been experienced before.

But, as regards all the new public access technologies, including news and entertainment, there will be some very real concerns inherent in these new digital devices. In addition to the obvious fears of counterfeit reproduction, there will be a growing concern about "falsification". Modern electronic piano keyboards use digitally recorded sounds. That is they "sample" the desired audio note which is in turn played back when the key is pressed. Using that technique, a hundred dollar keyboard can simulate the sound of a Steinway grand piano with appropriate audio amplification and acoustics. In a variation of this system, it is possible to "sample" handwriting and produce "average" alphabet letters to write documents that are not actual "copies" of any prior document and yet are visibly accurate handwriting. There is also a technology developing that derives from Artificial Intelligence technology. This new equipment digitalizes facial expressions. In a related effort, the technology actually reads lips. Equipment of this kind has enormous potential for helping language students, stroke victims, paralysis patients, and many others to achieve accelerated progress. It will be easy to produce cartoons of well known personalities actually speaking in a synthesized voice which is identical to the person and displaying the person's facial patterns. All the same, using the exact same science, it will also be possible to reproduce the facial movements of library file video's and have the modified video appear to be voicing opinions, with synchronized audio and visual, which were never actually uttered by the person. In other words, it will become possible to realistically produce a counterfeit video of a fundamentalist minister preaching evolution in his own voice and with his own facial expressions! Talk about identity theft!

[9]The initial entertainment industry concern was the anticipated competition of television and the Internet. An emerging certainty is that the two modes will go beyond complementary to being inter-active. Motion picture distributors already are producing web sites not only advertising pictures being screened at local theaters, but even pre-selling admissions. The television producers are increasingly using e-mail for on-program audience feedback and will start using Internet chat room to include an audience larger than their studio audience to enhance the drama of their programs. Interactive television programs respond to the new era paradigm of personal choice expression which will produce an augmented experience for the viewer and, very likely, an instructive input for the program producers which is going to affect advertising, content, and even politi-

cal policies. For local cable broadcasts it will open new sources of local business revenue and government feedback on subjects of local tastes, and priorities. It is reasonable to expect that future digital television receivers will even be equipped with a "mouse' much in the manner of a personal computer while, at the same time, programming will be developed with "hyper content". Viewers will be able to "point" at something of interest and effortlessly be directed to web sites for further information. If the viewer is interested in a particular product, the material appears on screen with promotional information, and without any need for viewer computer expertise. Such technology, available on home television sets will change the political and merchandizing processes of America in some very electrifying fundamentals. It might also put many salesmen out of work.

This kind of television will give viewers the real opportunity for participation and involvement which distinctly makes being a couch potato a choice not a condition. In the future, digital television will, in a very real way, merge the purpose of personal computers including their enormous capacity for storing information, with the television experience with its vast ability to disseminate information. The combination will be further enhanced by voice recognition technology which will ultimately reduce even the biblical "Tower of Babel" burden of language of both. It will combine the audience of computer savvy people who are perfectly comfortable with technology, with the more numerous, and therefore more commercially important passive viewer who never programs his VCR—again with benefits to both. That amalgamation of such disparate audiences is possibly going to be one of the more unexpected consequences of new era digital entertainment.

Summary:

Twenty-first century equipment will not only transform *how* we entertain ourselves, it will radically accommodate where and when we do it, as well as who sources that activity. Early in this period commercial, popularly priced equipment will offer selection of any music, film, or information program of choice on several hundred channels all of which will become interactive. Combined with the already interactive electronic network, this will permit extensive shopping, conversations, research of medical, literary, performances, travel and weather around the world, as well as myriad other information's, all at the touch of a button, or at voice command, that will replace TV remotes and a mouse.

That same level of programming will become available, most likely with political resistance, all over the world and that will produce something of a dilemma.

Electronic newspapers, books, magazines, and courses are already available, almost all of them having an online version. In the relatively near future software will permit "voice to print" transposition and "print to voice" transposition, albeit for an often used (limited) vocabulary, with probable inter-language translation, again for that limited vocabulary, so that you will be able to "hear" your news reports or classroom dialog regardless of origin without the "benefit" of official translation. It will become possible to provide international sales or exchanges of homes, art, vacations, and even recipes personally and directly between the interested parties.

While entertainment is broadly regarded as the manner in which a society relaxes, in a global economic world, it inadvertently takes on a much more serious role. Entertainment becomes the public representation of the values and ethics of the nation which will obviously be on view for the entire world. It is the lens through which the rest of the world perceives and judges us—warts and all. Films are among our major exports which not only generate profits and jobs for Americans, they tell people who have no other knowledge of us who we are and what we value. There was a time that that kind of information could be filtered through the local rulers but just as technology will make virtually any information easily available to Main Street, modern technology will probably make it almost as accessible to Shanghai Street in spite of any government objections. This will be further impacted by the increasing capacity of entertainment as an interactive media. When the man on Main Street is able to "talk back" to any content providers, they will obviously be able to "talk with" fellow content receivers and the distance between Main Street and Shanghai Street will shrink. Hopefully, that will positively influence the residents at both ends of the connection. In that sense entertainment on demand acquires national significance because it presents the opportunity for foreign nationals, as well as Americans to go past two dimensional stereotypes. I suspect that fundamentalist nations, for example, might not all like what they see.

Reading and Reference:

[1] *Newsweek* 1/1/2000

[2] AJC October 18, 2001

[3] AJC April 18, 2002

[4] *IEEE Spectrum* July 2002

[5] *Time Magazine* May 22, 2000

[6] *Global Television* Schneider and Wallis 0 262 69123 X

[7] *The Economist* Sept. 21, 2002

[8] *Probable Tomorrows* Cetron & Davies 0 312 15429 1

[9] *Essential Guide to Digital Set-top Boxes & Interactive TV*. G.O'Driscoll 0 13 017360 6

9

Networks—The Insular Association

For the Founding Fathers, personal freedom was so strong a sentiment, many of them including Madison, Jefferson, Franklin, Burr, and others, were "Deists"—i.e., people who were convinced God got the ball rolling in the beginning, and then withdrew from the field essentially leaving it to His human creation. If God intended freedom from even His restraint, they reasoned, humans should not presume to pre-empt His purpose subsequent to His creation.

Freedom had, in fact, never happened in history. Church, or State, or Church AND State always seemed to intercept any perception of His intent. In an effort to thwart that affiliation, an amendment to the Constitution specifically prohibits it. The Founder's initial conception of the new nation was a very loosely connected but cooperating confederation of the previous colonies. They even objected to a Federal bank because it might obstruct the individual state's right to issue its own money. They objected to a "national" army because it could override state militias. When they finally sat down to work it out, reality set in. What about inter-state commerce? Roads? Property? Trade? Currency? How about mutual defense? In the end, they jointly accepted a not-so-loose confederation but one with presumably clear cut individual rights among which were the absolute rights to privacy and to private property. The privacy stance was so strong even national identity cards have always, in the past, been roundly rejected. There were even political battles about draft cards. How about the future?

Those attitudes are already being seriously compromised, allegedly because of "war on terrorism" considerations but technology will continue to warp those traditions even after the war is won. Most, perhaps all financial transactions will use electronic money with a name on it. Eventually, as already noted, smart cards will include your driver's license, your bank account, your mortgage information, your medical data and history, your insurance data, your professional (and per-

156

haps private) memberships, your passport including your photograph, finger-print, retinal print, and travel history, and hardly least, all your credit card memberships, all of which might be on a single card. What makes all this technology practical is, of course, the twin phenomenon called "electronic networks" or the "Internet", and microprocessors. In 1990 very few people had ever heard of either one and far fewer had any conscious use of them. Of the handful of individuals who did use them, it is probably safe to say virtually none remotely thought the Internet would become globally operational within one decade.

If all the personal information which will be entered on those Smart Cards is un-nerving, consider the greater reality. [2]In the networked world all of it can be flashed around the entire world in seconds. Some have been argued all this "smart" credit card private data is your personal property. Others have characterized these networks as huge copying machines so transmitting unencrypted information is tantamount to tacit copying permission. It may sound a bit far fetched but the data is arguably on a public electronic highway and this is a public interest argument. Copyright laws were written before the advent of the Internet and the relationship of the two will become the subject of major legal challenges. The most recent example was a court case involving use of the Internet to distribute recorded—and copyrighted—music. The network technologies of the twenty-first century will impinge on so many traditional concepts of property and individual rights that court actions will be issued for conditions which never existed before. More than abstract conceptual "rights", those networks are going to change everyone's daily practice in very critical aspects.

The revolution is hard for some people to believe because as widespread as it already is, networking is not yet universally inclusive. In the near time, nobody will be exempted from its outreach. Technologies normally become widespread in the United States over a period of generations. Most people of the time never heard of a locomotive and indeed, some parts of Africa and Asia still, after two hundred years, have not been seen one. The automobile was practically a nuisance in the United States but within fifty years was spreading across the whole population. The airplane was almost a class distinction. Today it is hard to find someone who hasn't flown. Even the telephone was initially exceptional and is now included in almost all building codes around the developed world. All the previous communications advances were limited by money or politics, or language. The Internet is inexpensive and becoming even more so, almost out of political control, and with almost no language restrictions. That pragmatic will significantly affect global cultures including the American, and we are only at the beginning of the beginning.

The flow of network information around the world is driven by business needs where security needs are paramount in network operations. As an instant example of the complexity of this problem, banks handle credit cards in one location, clear checks in a second, and do data processing in a third. Colonial Management Associates is a nationwide accounting firm but does all of its data process in Denver. The modern currency market is the largest market in the world and it lives on electronic processing. Network commerce is so extensive it actually has a life of its own. As far back as 1977 the Society for Worldwide Inter-bank Financial Telecommunication (acronym "SWIFT") became the world's largest international electronic network. (It is now far exceeded by the Internet.) SWIFT, as a system, connected the banking systems of over 100 nations. This network has become so immense it has become virtually impossible to control money nationally. It has been estimated that the currency movement via the Internet in and out of the Chicago Mercantile Exchange exceeds the combined GDP of the entire world. All of this as a direct consequence of the electronic network facility which is, in effect, a twenty four hour seven day a week mall for any type of transaction. Networking is currently the hottest growth area for microprocessor development. Fiber optic transmission systems have actually overbuilt this capacity (a contributing reason for the 2002 stock market drop) in anticipation of the international networked market. The world business electronic network has gone far beyond mere money. It even deals in barters.

It is important, for starters, to understand the difference between the "World Wide Web" and the Internet. The "WWW" is a vast and growing collection of individual locations (called "pages") where one can find specific information about specific subjects. Web pages are "clustered" around what is called "Servers". People can have personal pages. Companies have them. Governments and government departments have them. The Internet is the means of reaching those pages by connecting to their servers. In that sense, the Internet is a train track to the express stops, the Servers. The Web pages are the local stations. Just to complete this description, there are two other terms of interest. Those are "Search Engines" and "Browsers". A search engine helps you locate Servers which host Web pages of interest and in a way, a Search Engine is itself is a Web site such as Yahoo whereas a browser is software you install on your own computer such as Netscape Navigator, to open Web pages.

Doing business over the Internet does not preclude the traditional need for business travel. Like every other category of customer, the business traveler has special needs. The business man usually can't anticipate trips far in advance. He might need to get somewhere immediately or might not even have a current passport. The State Department maintains a Web site which can be accessed via the Internet anywhere in the connected world for help, instructions, application forms, as well as the closest source of assistance and location of embassies or consuls. In spite of all the fears of "government data bases", positive I.D. data on "smart" credit cards will permit instant identification and virtually instant passport production. The Department Web site includes Travel Advisories and Warnings detailing the hazards of the intended locations. Also, in this regard, the CIA, usually secretive about everything, has a Web site which publishes unclassified information about nearly every country in the world and this too is already instantly available and expanding. (Sad to say, in a era in which the world is so connected, "Terrorism" initiated by the few, makes these aspects of the Internet important features.) In spite of the American aversion to ID cards, Smart Cards with such information will eventually enter the culture prompted by such considerations as terrorist control.

[2]Business people will be able to book most of their other needs—including ground transportation, flyer points, entertainment, and even cash—and will book or confirm all trip plans via the net, from wherever they are. There are even special features aimed at traveling business women. The net contains features such as local customs, local maps, restaurants, and prohibitions helpful to the frequent traveler. Most important, all of this will be expanded to wireless modem laptops, protected cell phones, and other wireless devices where connectivity with the office is at the end of your fingers and this will become available in ever expanding access in the immediate future. These devices, able to accomplish all of these functions, will shrink to pocket dimensions with simple operation eliminating the need for computers even to receive e-mail. Many of them will include translation dictionaries as well as Global Positioning features not only telling you where you are in strange neighborhoods and foreign lands, but how to get to where you are going.

Terrorism might be a millennial scourge for awhile, perhaps even for a long while, but as history goes, it won't last indefinitely. On the other hand illness is more of an ordinary problem and here too the electronic networks are changing the world permanently. The U.S. government operates a Web site controlled by the CDC (Center for Disease Control) which posts current information concerning health conditions, food and water safety, atmospheric considerations, and indicated immunizations for every country in the world. Random Access Memory (RAM) technologies are improving so rapidly that in the very near future pocket sized internet devices will include a medical "what to do" program for most geographic locations which will also access CDC, or other medical resources, emergency facilities, as well as your own doctor almost instantaneously. The U.S. State Department also operates a Web site which lists local medical resources around the world. And there are more of these health oriented electronic network assets coming on line as we write.

In the nomadic world of the twenty-first century, all the above will provide additional facility for mobility. It won't be intimidated by fanatics and it won't be restricted to vacations. Many think the combination of extremely easy communications, a global stock market, and super-rapid electronic fund transfers are going to make bottom line considerations limit vacations and challenge the necessity for the frequent business trips of the twentieth century. It may very well be true but the betting is that traveling will increase not decrease and for this purpose the e-network resources are perfectly adapted and expanding.

[2]By 1995 the software allowed virtually any semi-literate person with the right equipment, to access the enormous accumulation of Web sites via the Internet. Public interest was so broad that within a few years, long established companies with reputations came to depend on the network Web sites for competitive survival. New public issues involving network technology were instant successes regardless of earnings, and in fact, these issues were in large part the driving force for the 90's stock market "bubble". Yahoo, a brand new search engine, was getting nearly five thousand new Web site submissions every day. Bill Gates, the founder of Microsoft and touted to be the richest man in the world at age forty, announced Microsoft would make the Internet market the central issue of his company. What was vital about this brand new market was that having originated as a military technology, it evolved into a business technology, and was proceeding to becoming a predominantly consumer resource. The Internet gave personal expression to anyone at all who had the need or just the desire to be heard. The complex serves the public pocket, their need, and their ego in a manner no other product or process has ever done. The public recognized it at a breathtaking speed. In the mid ninety's Internet participation doubled every two months. There are now hundreds of millions of people interconnected without the benefit of clergy (government) or borders. What started as an upscale, white collar market now covers the spectrum of collars. It is probably no exaggeration to observe every application, questionnaire, survey, exam, or anything else, already contains the question "e-mail address?". And again, it all happened in about a decade.

As enormous as the world e-network has grown to be, wireless system connection is adding new dimensions. For an unlimited network, being restricted to tethered location connection is a conflict in concept. Cell phones are so omnipresent the running joke is some day cell phones will need to be surgically separated from their owners. The number of residential hardwired phones is actually declining for the first time in more than seventy five years. The cell phone spread has reached the point people are beginning to use their cell phone in place of hardwired phones rather than as an addition. They are not only more convenient, they are more economical and, for the most part, people can be reached with the same number regardless of their physical location, en route, or long distance. In any case the competition developing for future markets is less between computer manufacturers, than it is between computers and cell phones. The split vision is the distinction of a computer in every home and one in every pocket. Dell Company, the worlds largest computer manufacturer has launched a series of hand held computers and mobile phone style computers. These phone based computers, beginning to be called "smart phones", have the computing power of PCs of only one decade ago!

[2]This competition is more compelling than a mere packaging concept difference. The hand held computer manufacturers believe in reducing their size to hand held pocket dimensions while the smart phone people subscribe to the idea of expanding the utility of cell phones to computing even including GPS location capacity. [1]In fact, the most recent technology is called "Nanotechnology' and will reduce computer sizes to almost pinpoint dimensions by using molecular computers for the active elements. In terms of a mobile phone, it might actually be a significant innovation for an industry which already claims over a billion subscribers around the world. What is fascinating about these two approaches, is not so much their differences as their consensus of the future. A pocket computer that can communicate externally is an inversion of a pocket telephone which can compute. Both are functionally approaching the same basic vision from opposite directions. The winner might not be determined as much by technology as by economics. PCs are going to become very common household equipment but PC sales have leveled off and without doubt, are being stunted by cell phone sales while cell phone sales are being energized by computer capability. In acknowledgement, Microsoft has changed its motto from the famous "**PC in every home**" to "**Empowering people through software any time, any place, for any device**". The mobile phone future has the advantage of a world largely without telephone (or much of any other kind) of infrastructure and so a market virtually without limits. In addition, the PC world is dominated by Microsoft and its "closed system" constraint on innovation. In contrast, the cell phones have, as yet, no similar limitation.

It is easy to understand the advantages of wireless connections for mobile communications but wireless networking for modern health monitors and crisis telemetry is crucial. Automatic cardiac monitoring, only as a single example, is now being developed in a number of modes, including cell phones. There is much more activity in this field than most people, even most doctors, realize. Welch Allyn Protocol, Agilent Technologies, Symbol Technologies, SpaceLabs Medical, Criticare Systems, Lucent Technologies, and many other companies are actively in the field of wireless medical applications. The market is much larger than the home monitoring field. Monitors of these types will be built into hospital rooms, assisted living homes, and nursing homes, with the readouts being fed to a remote central panel instead of to individual nursing stations on each floor of each institution. The central panel need not and probably will not, be geographically local or even continentally local. Indeed there has been discussion of establishing a "world monitor" with guaranteed expertise provided for third world and low capability facilities very much in the same context of remote controlled surgery already spreading. Medical telemetry is becoming so imminent the FCC is developing a number of assigned frequency bands specifically reserved for medical purposes. There is anticipation a world wide conference will probably soon occur to set up world wide standards for medical data transfer in order to minimize the possibility of interference.

For such purpose, network security is a problem almost on a par with interference. Even if the effort to guard network data and to ensure privacy is almost totally successful there will always remain the nagging fear of gate crashers, but the potential benefits to risk ratio, in medical terms, is so large the conversion to network medicine is well under way. Personal information security is obviously a serious issue but for medical service, economics is a more difficult issue. All of these network connecting equipments involve a great deal of money and this technology is developing so fast that system life time is not nearly as problematic as system obsolescence. In simple language, equipment maintenance systems won't be a problem because a good deal of it won't be in service long enough to fail. Furthermore, service suppliers might not be able to depreciate equipment before they are forced to replace "old" systems with "new" ones. In most technologies, costs tend to come down as they age but these are changing so fast that ageing is fast going below the radar horizon for medical and incidentally commercial gear as well. Like analog to digital TV, the replacement aspect may be the greatest hurdle. In spite of impediments, within the next decade most people will be using wireless Internet service and almost as many will be using wireless network communications for their personal as well as medical needs. There are simply too many direct rewards and incidental fringe benefits including the economy of installation. Wireless systems are very adaptable. Unlike copper wire systems, wireless is broadband, i.e., fast. They move when you move. New customers are easy to add without significant introduction of additional facility and you don't need to dig up streets to add capacity. Wireless is going to be a dominating system within a very few years and this is one of the few point blank forecasts made in this volume.

[23] In yet another aspect of wireless networking, it is important to realize that most of the American housing plant was produced prior to the computer revolution. Where originally there was a single computer for every home which purchased computers, now there are at least two, and where there are children involved, there are more than two. Hardwired interconnection is not only expensive, it is difficult. Wireless is developing even faster as a connection media. Eventually, the wireless connection will permit data transmission rates in excess of 54 mb/s (megabytes per second) and they will come in a dizzying variety of packages and capabilities including wireless data networking, high speed local area networks, multimedia local area networks, voice and data transmission, and wireless communication for homes.

[1]Networks will be everywhere and envelop every activity both evident and unseen. As an example microchips are becoming so powerful and so inexpensive they are expected to be included in structural designs such as buildings and bridges to detect failures before they happen, in farm fields to detect weather and soil conditions, in pharmacy to detect medical conditions,—all them ultimately connected through the Internet. Perhaps the most visible applications will be in the areas of news, entertainment, and education. In an era convulsing as much as this one, the news of the moment is probably more important than ever before. After all these years, the world is still legislating boundaries for print, radio, and television media and the Internet combines all three with the radical complication of personal interactivity.

[2]The original news source, a newspaper, was slow and was already "old" when you read it. However, it was usually a detailed report. Television invited family participation, and literally allowed vivid "reader" observation *in color*, and in real time as the event unfolded. Of course, as broadcast news became sponsored, broadcast news famously began to resemble entertainment more than news. You had to sit through many segments including Hollywood gossip in which you might have no interest and often had to sift through single sided approaches. The latest game in town is the Internet on which you will eventually find almost any writer of public note, and quite a few of self assumed note. You

will assemble your own paper from papers and magazines, or any publication almost anywhere in the world, and have it delivered to your home via your computer on the very day of publication. At this point, real time digital network reports, like TV stories, are rarely as detailed as newsprint narratives, but it too is changing and the future will bring images, both moving and still, to further enhance the on-line story.

Internet news reader will also defeat the unredeemable sin of the news business—imitation. It is often hard to distinguish news sources of any description because in this remarkably competitive business they all pretty much pick the same stories to push. (Of course, the obverse of this negative is that on-line newspapers, assembled by the reader permit him to pick and choose sources as well as stories, i.e., "filter" his reading material—perhaps, in the long run, not such a great benefit.) Still, realistically speaking, that avenue is already open to him with newsprint as well as TV sources. Furthermore, the print media is a one way conversation i.e., one person addressing many. In contrast, the Internet is interactive. Digital newspapers will become more like a "debate" than a lecture. The reader can "talk back" to the writer. In fact, assembling his electronic network paper actually *encourages* the reader (relatively effortlessly) to correspond with the journalist, a detail which might actually be an inducement to read what the other side has to say. Reporters might tend to become somewhat more cautious because of this completely novel experience of intimate contact with diverse readers. Electronic reporting should also become more accurate because the network is a real time, twenty four hour, seven day a week phenomenon. It is literally up to the minute. When a newspaper goes to bed, it prints the last Dow-Jones numbers. Electronic newspapers print the D-J at the moment of issue. In a turbulent world, which this is apt to be, and with so many pension funds, such a distinction will be vital. In addition on-line news moderates any restrictive local character because the network is global, so its readership will be potentially global—and the interactivity is also global. That induces in regional papers an expanded national potential they don't otherwise enjoy. It might also be a safe bet that the new Internet journalism will diminish the twentieth century "mass media" concept because this form of information invites catering to more narrow interests. This would really become an unexpected consequence.

Far more people use the Internet than use the library. As a matter of fact digitally stored material will very soon far outstrip the total content of paper storage in all those libraries. Material stored digitally can be updated almost instantly without throwing anything away, whereas obsolete books can only be thrown away. Considering the downward trend of computer prices, many school and library systems are beginning to suspect the provision of students with laptop computers and CD ROM's might be cheaper in the long run than supplying books which, in a time of such brisk change, are almost inevitably and often quickly obsolete. The CD ROM serves a simultaneous long term utilitarian computer training purpose. Public Libraries can now be accessed via the Internet to make reservations for book loans, but the library growth industry of the future will be books on demand much as the entertainment mode of the future will be programs on demand. Internet Public Libraries are already springing up with exactly this modality. Library Science courses are being explored specifically focused on Internet style libraries. For grade school students the Internet Libraries will not only offer practice in using computers and the Internet, it will teach them the enormous information content existing on the network and how to access it—knowledge which will be vital to their later careers almost independent of what career they chose. The growth of electronic library facilities underlines the value of grade school computer courses in an age when inability to use it disables even the use of a conventional library. There may be no emotional analogy between curling up with a good book and sitting down with a monitor, but most people don't actually own many books while in the very near future, most families will own computers, much as they now own television sets. As a matter of fact, as television digitalizes, their TV sets will serve as functional computers making video books available in homes which have never seen a paper book.

[2]The changes won't be limited to the printed page. Television programming will be affected in a manner very similar to the way radio audiences were affected by the advent of television. As audience share shifted from radio to television, so did advertising revenue. However, the television broadcasters were, for the most part, the very same companies which broadcast radio. They had the audience, the experience, and the performer contracts to accomplish the conversion and simply segment the outlets. Radio became "talk radio" and music broadcast. It seems to have found its niche. Television rapidly acquired all the dynamics of a growth industry for news, theater, soap operas, and public access. The limitation was space—called "spectrum". There just wasn't enough of it so the number of channels was very limited. Cable TV partially solved the problem of spectrum because programming was transmitted over private cables not public airways. The FCC (Federal Communications Commission) actually had no jurisdiction since there was no interference with other forms of communication. The ability to generate carrier frequencies for many channels, like so many other technologies of which we are speaking, was only a matter of time, and not much time. Cable TV, in almost no time, overtook commercial broadcast TV, and pretty quickly, the

broadcast TV programs were being watched in far greater numbers on cable than from "rabbit ears". With many more channels, cable TV could generate much more program material (no license and, of course, more revenue) but by this time much of it was created by independent producers. It implied more variety so the new material blended well with the new age expansion of personal choices. The cable technology also encouraged an expansion of local interest programming including area politics, religion, etc.

However, with it all, the basic program format remained pretty much the same—program material during specific time slots, with advertising interlaced between program slots. But, modern recording and remote control technology is making sponsor evasion easy. "Channel surfing" is an every day affair with the understanding that the real boss of the household was "he who controlled the remote". However, advertising will remain a major revenue source for the industry—the only reason, in fact, that both the broadcast companies and the producing companies are in the business. Audience material control is fostering very novel changes in the promotion techniques such as introducing "the message" as an integral part of the program. Instead of having a Ford Motor Company advertisement sponsoring a James Bond picture on television, James Bond might be shown conspicuously driving a Ford car. This is actually a great change which will become more prevalent in the early part of this next era, but where it will go is still speculative.

In contrast, Internet programming is not restricted to time slots nor is advertising sandwiched between program fragments. Even more attention-grabbing, the advertiser's message is often directly interspersed spatially with the program material. Furthermore, attracted customers can respond or place orders directly and immediately, through hyper text, to the sponsor who can then relay the order to the closest, most convenient outlet. It additionally gives the advertiser the mechanism for immediate feedback both as regards customer interest, and, very important, ad effectiveness. The technology already includes polls, color, text, cartoons and sound. Like both radio and TV before, the learning curve will continue to improve action, sound and presentation generally, including audience interaction not yet conceived. All of it has a great potential for commerce and commercials which means the print media, broadcast TV, radio, and now even cable TV will have some real competition for advertising money—the life blood of all four.

Selling by Internet will be cheap compared to newsprint, and will reach a much larger audience. It will probably be more effective than the previously conventional media advertisements, which is why the conventional media is going on line as an adjunct to their publication. As an example, newspaper and TV stations cannot accurately report to a sponsor on how many people actually were attracted by an ad. Because of the Internet interactivity, online advertisements do a much better reporting job. While TV advertisements have time "spots", digital advertisements, like printed papers have no time element. Internet sales probably exceed four billion dollars, and at the moment are not taxed because, among other reasons, there is no agreement on the appropriate taxing agency, if, for example, the customer or the seller is overseas.

[2]Like television, the Internet will eventually be accessible to one and all. And it will have some unanticipated outcomes. For years American parents have watched in dismay as their children spent more and more time in front of television screens and proportionately less time in front of a book, the realistic fear being that TV diminishes their reading ability. The Internet forces them to read. In fact, reading is once again an "in" activity although subject matter is becoming another concern. That is still not implanting the love of books, but it does, at least, allow for improvement. Moreover, if inadequate reading skills have been a prime complaint, absent civic skills were another. The growing requirement for computer competence is forcing schools to encompass computers as part of their basic teaching equipment and inclusion will inescapably engender wider use of digital newspapers as part of school programs. Also in the category of progress is the self motivating factor of immigrants, and particularly immigrant children, learning English in order to enjoy the broadest rewards of the Internet. There are, of course, no prohibitions of ethnic activities on the Internet, but from an adolescent's point of view, the possibilities in English far outweigh those in any other language.

A further addition to the global network theme will be video games. For the moment, most video games are computer supported, i.e., the games require a PC with a hard disc and a CD ROM accessory. In the future, the PC itself will probably become nothing more than a terminal and the games will be Internet interactive. It will be easy to set up a poker game in which all the players are baby-sitting in their own homes. Those homes won't necessarily be on the same continent. Here again, most games are in English, a further incentive for foreign born children to make the crossover.

Industry estimates guess that at the turn of the millennium, there were over one hundred million Americans and better than twenty million young people with access to computers. Surveys indicated nine out of ten of the youngsters have used word processors, six out of ten have done Internet research for school work, and more than half of them have sent e-mail. The Internet is a media which, like the old silent motion pictures of the twenties, offers everyone, regardless of race, creed, language, or location, ghetto or upscale, city or farm, able or disabled—everyone—an opportunity to learn and to share their ideas, their problems, and even their games and amusements. Maybe the kids will finally do more for international understanding than their parents could.

Real choice, however, must include freedom from interception and the "privacy issue" will become a very widespread problem. It isn't only the computer networks which are involved in privacy issues. Video cameras at road intersections, in factories and offices, in public buildings, in public gathering places will be as omnipresent as they have always been in banks but much less obvious. Eavesdropping on any phones is so widespread there is a widespread fear in Europe (probably with cause) Americans are listening in on their business calls. With grounds or without, that makes life a bit more paranoid. E-network's use will soon be so widespread as to be ubiquitous. The networks can often, unless the service is somehow shielded, identify not only the user, but the use itself. Already routinely employed by many, the networks will soon literally be exploited by all, for all the social, financial, medical, business, political, and personal purposes discussed in this volume. Without some very strong technical safeguards in addition to legal protection, all the data will permit many providers including cable companies and servers to develop extensive pictures of individual life styles. From a commercial position it is awesome information. From a personal point of view, it is an invasion of privacy. And from a legal point of view, it's probably unconstitutional.

In spite of all the problems of the moment, the business advantages of networks and the proliferation of computers has driven the Internet to become as basic a business parameter as the telephone. It is used for ordering supplies, advertisement, catalogs, customer contact, sales, product support, and even the salesman's nirvana, customer "conversation". That last aspect will probably become, with time, the most important aspect of Internet transactions. As people become more relaxed with electronic sales, they will become more confident with its impersonality. However, catalogs alone don't often close sales and the Internet will become a very busy interactive connection. This is very important because in a competitive market prices will necessarily tend to be comparable. The closing factor for a sale becomes the interaction not only in terms of the product itself but also from the modern perspective of what has been called "mass customization". Products are mass produced but each one is personalized to the customer. In the same context of the new economy in which renting products and accessories will begin to outweigh selling them, the network can contribute to an ongoing business relationship through a twenty four hour, seven day service support system which is the basis of repeat sales.

On a more personal level, people will always want a feeling of community. "Community" implies people who share a set of standards; culture, language, and perhaps economic status. In short, communities usually share common lifestyles. Most conventionally, they share common geography. They are neighbors, friends, classmates, and not infrequently, related. They may not always agree within the area but they often have much the same world-view. The "them and us" perspective is precisely what the Internet will further corrode. Movies, radio and television moderately changed that construction because the outside world at least passively infringed on individual worlds on an occasional basis. An interactive world wide network will encroach in a much more personal manner because of the two way connection. People on line will be able to find much of that range of needs with individuals they might never actually know or meet. Their range of links might well be global, and without regard to race, religion, gender, disabilities, or even class. The bond of cyber friendships might be single issue or a spectrum but their members will be participants in many different communities, probably with different people, interests, or even age groups. The members will almost certainly have more variegated membership with mixed purpose, and certainly the potential for more sophisticated interests. Without doubt, cyber connections will provide the potential for opening vistas of affiliations most will never have otherwise experienced. This condition will be particularly functional in an age of loosening geographic ties and in which separation and loneliness will be more widespread, and lifestyles more frenetic.

For much the same reasons, the spreading use of the Internet to find soul mates will be the latest scheme of a very old quest. Twenty years ago, nobody would have believed computers would be as common as television sets in private homes. Ten years ago the notion of finding friends with a computer was inconceivable. Only a few years ago, the idea of looking for a mate on the computer was absolutely embarrassing. And yet, all of it has come to pass and Internet socializing of all kinds, in this impersonal time is obviously going to increase. Print "lonely hearts" columns are pretty traditional, in fact, common. In comparison, Internet connections will have some real advantages among which are economy of time and money as well as efficiency, but also some risks. The advantages already more than balance the risks because finding friends and potential mates through this route is outpacing the print media version. In a July, 2000 column the New York Times estimated that over 60% of American singles would look for dates on the Internet that year. Online matchmaking Web sites, and there are already hundreds of them and growing, are claiming a signup membership of something like ten million, which is certainly not to say anything about their success rate. Still, it's a sign of the times because such a high percentage weighs in on the failure of traditional means of church, work, blind dates, and even bars. Using the net lends itself to both anonymity and precision. For instance, one can spell out partialities such as physical characteristics, interests, religion, and age group. Politically incorrect requirements such as race, educational achievement, and party affiliation, can be specified without self consciousness. Responses can be appraised at leisure, even using "webcams" (i.e., camera's which transmit real time digital motion pictures via the Internet) without personal security risks. There need not be any initial exchange of telephone numbers, addresses, real names, or in fact, anything but e-mail conversations. If interest lacks or lapses, hitting the "delete" key ends the "relationship". The personal chemistry which is the object of most such searches can't be established electronically so the outcome is probably as often as not, disappointing. And of course the Internet offers no more protection from aberrational people than do bars. Once again, the significance of this latest way of match making is not the mechanics, i.e., not the fact that it uses a computer, but rather that it conforms to the circumstance of the portable culture of the time.

In general, Internet friendships can be very close to inscrutability and while the anonymity can be penetrated, it takes more determination than most cyber space participants are willing or able to deliver. For some, concealment turns out to be a license because secrecy permits a level of "adventure" that they might otherwise be unwilling to hazard. Such connections are particularly a-propos for "communities of strangers" with perhaps, only a single point of commonality. One can even be a member of the group—an "observer" so to speak—without participating in any of its activities. A very fair example of this premise of "a community of strangers" is the level of Internet political chat in China which is notably lacking in public discourse. The Internet has become controversially active in China for the same reason. The Chinese government recognizes the valuable economic opportunities presented by the e-network while recognizing the real political dangers of a widespread information technology. They have tried to restrict "dangerous" Web sites and e-mail, with limited success. As an interesting illustration of their fruitless efforts, the Fourth World Conference on Women took place in Beijing in 1995, but included inputs of women actually not attending as well as those present. They used e-mail and network conferencing, as well as the World Wide Net to produce the first geographically dispersed international conference of its kind in history—certainly the most unique experience in communist Chinese history. Over one hundred thousand visits were made to their Web site. Despite great efforts, the government of China was essentially unable to control those world wide communication links.

But the coin will have an obverse side. For all the interactivity, the network is aloof. Anonymity permits participants to establish semi-fictional biographies with seemingly appropriate feedback from their Internet "friends". And there lie the problems and risks. For instance, the Internet doesn't recognize geography so respondents can turn out to be continents apart (sometimes considered an advantage). People using such distant resort might be perfectly functional but lacking in either social confidence or grace. False personas are usually disclosed only after the Internet "dates" gives way to actual dates. Research conducted in 1995 (Parks and Floyd) and again in 1999 (Mckenna and Bargh) confirms that internet friendships were more intimate but also more illusory and that they formed more quickly than face to face friendships. The new electronic friends may not necessarily be added to one's "old friends". By developing new and conceivably more exotic electronic social contacts, particularly in a context of weakening local ties, interactive networks can be a factor for a greater degree of detachment from people actually participating in their lives. The idea was suggested in a study in 1998 (Kraut, Patterson, et al) where they found that using the Internet as little as two hours a week correlated with a loss of local associations and conversely, an increase in "non-local" friendships. (The Mckenna and Bargh 1999 study pointed out most of those who had formed Internet friendships did subsequently meet "in the flesh" so the clock might still be ticking on this subject.) Still, even radio and TV churches tend to divert attachment from local institutions, so Internet associations might become a factor in reducing the shared regional experiences which are traditionally so vital to a sense of geographic community. In addition, home offices, home schooling, in combination with the pursuit of electronic friends around the world, all in aggregate, undermine the skills of co-mingling with random group diversity. For all of those reasons, network "friends" will likely be more impermanent. Changing chat groups is easier than changing neighbors if, as is always the case, the association hits a rough spot.

While bridging the dichotomy between virtual relations and face to face relations is going to require major social constructs, the action means are at hand. Just as cable TV introduced the viability of community channels, a limitless network is permitting the existence of community Web pages and community chat groups where it is possible for local citizens to connect with each other and remain informed of local events. Neighborhood chat groups will direct at least some electronic friendships to the local area amenities where there is a direct convergence of interests and a real contact opportunity for people socializing. In this society where a stranger is simply the last person to arrive, these kinds of programs will encourage participation, and community activity. It is very likely that with time, towns will provide free Internet access services in post-offices, libraries, police and fire stations, senior centers, and even city halls. In areas where such advantages were established, some towns have progressed to the point of scheduled meetings and activities so network camaraderie might be merged into personal friendships. And the very same facilities will be used to introduce isolated individuals and new arrivals to local churches, civic activities, schools, and theaters. Until very recently, computer know-how was pretty much limited to well to do, educated young people. It is interesting to observe that it has graduated to a social asset for the whole community. Pocket computers, digital TV set-tops, and "smart cell phones" will further magnify this asset value.

The information age, for the poor, will be both a new opportunity and another limitation unless public access to the networks becomes a common community facility. About twenty five percent of Americans are under the poverty line, have no bank accounts, own no homes, and certainly, no computers. With immigration rates rising, that percentage is likely to increase. The poor are essentially disconnected from the American social process, but they do have families and personal associations. Most of them want jobs and in this phase, the Internet will be one of the best ways to find them. For them, technology will be a boon if it is accessible to them. Several studies have shown usage of the Internet for job hunting correlates almost directly with service accessibility but the Department of Commerce reports less than fifteen percent of Americans with an income of less than fifteen thousand dollars have computer access. The figure for families with incomes of over seventy five thousand is about eighty percent.

Those figures are an important demonstration of why Internet access is going to be driven to increase substantially in the early millennial period. Some research has indicated poor people with network access actually use the resource for more than job hunting. The statistical evidence is that low income people are actually more likely than high income people to use the Internet for studying on-line courses from English and American culture to job skills. This data added to the argument of population mobility suggests that the demand for public network access, like the original demand for public telephone access, is likely to become a mandated national requirement very soon. Just as there is a cost built into all hardwired telephone bills to provide universal telephone service, so it is likely there will soon be some funding for universal Internet access which will likely include wireless entry devices. There are several early indications of this development among Western nations. The Vancouver (Canada) Housing Authority, through an arrangement with the Vancouver school district, the country and the city, as well as several neighborhood citizens associations, is sponsoring the installation of high speed wiring and an installed computer in each housing unit. It has also set up learning centers in the school to train the residents in their use. This plan is already showing signs of both success and expansion using libraries and schools for public access stations. There are similar efforts growing here in the United States. In July of 2000, "One Economy Corp." with help from several other U.S. companies including AOL assembled a plan to work with public housing authorities to provide renting residents with computers, Internet access, and training in English and Spanish, which permit them to acquire network provided information on such subjects as healthcare, jobs, bank loans, and educational resources. The IBA Community Development Corp. of Boston has developed a project which will introduce Internet access to a low income community in Boston. Other communities around the country are working with the Fannie Mae foundation to make the Internet available to residents, and particularly to children, who might not otherwise be exposed to modern technology and as a result, be shut out. It may still be too early to make success or failure judgments, but it is evident the Internet will become one of the new era's best approaches to reducing poverty. This blueprint is in the process of very rapid escalation as computers and computer dexterity becomes ever more vital.

Unfortunately, from a community perspective, network interactivity gives participants with anti-social incentives the same ability to assemble, i.e., find people (and ideas) with which they can identify while at the same time being shielded from contrast. People out of the mainstream easily find others of similar warp and are therefore able to assemble local groups which reinforce each other's ego and potentially, support each other's hostilities. Web sites open new opportunities for hate groups. The sites will continue to be used to find and recruit new members. There are extremist Web sites of almost any description encompassing anti-Semitic, racist, and homophobic, including the Ku Klux Klan. The Internet has created many first amendment issues which will tested in the near term. Aside from violating any local or state ordinances, such activities will come under the purview of the accumulating anti-terrorism legislation, at the very least, and that too will become another Internet "freedom of speech" question requiring resolution very soon.

The Internet is such an alluring objective for non-ideological lawbreakers as well as the merely mischievous for the very reasons of speed, anonymity, and accessible. So far, in this very young technology, hackers, often adolescents, have been able to penetrate the CIA Web site which raised fears of national policy impairment. Hackers have attempted to flood Capital Hill with junk e-mail, create traffic jams on the system, and shut down the Florida 911 system. Any computer in any location can be used for deviant purposes if the user is computer savvy. Viruses have originated in Indonesia where the American authorities have no access to perpetrators. This kind of activity is threatening enough that a Commission on Critical Infrastructure Protection was established specifically to anticipate those dangers in order prevent them from disrupting an American century increasingly vulnerable to shielded remote sabotage.

Network crime is of recent vintage only because the networks themselves are new phenomenon. There is no controlling agency as regards "truth in advertising". It is not really easy to protect the consumer from fraud because like viruses, Web pages can originate from almost anywhere. This condition is actually coming somewhat under control, at least nationally. The Federal Government has prosecuted fraud cases in cooperation with state governments and they have shut down Web sites committing fraud but fraud and theft is easier to identify. Pornography originating in a country in which it is legal, makes stopping it more problematical. Libel is another example of a hard to make case for Internet prosecution. It might be possible to sue an Internet server for the sins of an author but it might be like holding a radio station responsible for the statements of a politician.

Personal Information has become very valuable, and unfortunately, with the enormous growth of ATM's, personal checks, credit cards, Internet banking, and so on, unauthorized information from more victims has also become more easily acquired. As a result, "identity theft", which is a form of theft by electronics, has become serious enough to be a separately identified crime with serious consequences if the perpetrator is caught. Banking networks, business networks, and even entertainment networks have been found by investigators to be most secure, while the news networks were least secure. It has been estimated that hackers alone have cost business worldwide about a billion dollars in 1995 and growing since then. This estimate is probably low because most companies will not report criminal break-ins of their network for fear of frightening customers. Security has become a major business because of all the above. For the most part security systems are improving. Serious thought is being given to enacting laws which permit computers to launch disabling attacks on computers which are identified as initiating viruses. The latter course opens grave international debate because those perpetrating criminal doings are not necessarily located within national borders.

Nevertheless, the greatest threat of illegal activity will be terrorism, which will most likely be international in both source and consequence.

Efforts at the control of international Web based crime are on the increase. In 1996, the G7/P8 group (Britain, France, Germany, Italy, Russia, the U.S., and Canada) came to an agreement in Paris on general rules to combat terrorist activities including several Internet measures. The Organization for Economic Cooperation and Development (OECD) and the European Union as well as nations within the Union have attempted to impose controls on the use of Internet for terrorism. Considering the events of September 11, an event which appears to have been coordinated by the Internet, all measures to date, were ineffective. Germany alone seems to have had some small degree of success by passing laws which, in effect, make the service providers responsible for the content of their clients. Throughout history, information has been regarded as a dangerous commodity with censorship the usual outcome. Even printing the bible was prohibited in some places and times. Newspapers, radio programs, and television are all under some level of control. The Internet is the first media in history which seems to defy restraint and the challenge has looming potential from both the crime prevention and the civil rights points of view.

Terrorism is not novel in history, unfortunately, but networks enable terrorists to easily communicate information more directly than at any previous time. Internet mail is quickly distributed and much more difficult to block. Fearing cell phone intercepts, the Al Qaeda is believed to be using the Internet to coordinate their followers around the world. Socially damaging use of the Internet has no simple "flag". Not to make any equivalence, pornography, which is also becoming an Internet distribution problem, is a good simile. Checking all internet correspondence is not only illegal for constitutional reasons, it is also difficult. China and every other totalitarian country are trying to control this traffic. Nevertheless, the great threat of terrorism will most likely be extra-national in both source and consequence and there will be increasing attention to this subject in the very near term.

Less than a single decade ago, communicating with someone across national borders was very expensive, and, to say the least, unpredictable. The e-network has reversed this circumstance in this remarkably short period of time. E-mail has become the means of preference to millions of people because it serves all the communication functions of conventional mail (called "snail mail"), is actually more convenient, instantaneous to any location in the world, *and* cheaper. That this is true is attested by e-mail as the primary inclusion of "smart phones". The recipient need not be attending his computer (or television set top adapter, or pocket device) because the letter, in effect, is deposited in his personal electronic mail box to be read at his convenience. When the wireless modems become widespread, only a matter of time, there will be a contact transformation with very large political and social repercussions around the world. Indeed e-mail communication will become available in parts of the world that don't yet have paved roads. As noted, the dictatorships are already having problems monitoring wired e-mail. Intercepting wireless modems will be an even greater hurdle for them because while computer based Internet messages are based on a single platform controlled by Microsoft, cell phones use many platforms. Ideas will have much more free access as will information, both technical and political. The ultimate certainty is that controlling the free flow of ideas in closed societies is becoming impossibly difficult.

The growth of the World Wide Web network has been so rapid as to have no precedent with which to gauge the future social import to individuals. In an epoch crammed with scientific advances, the e-net is truly unparalleled. Soon, electronic network influence will far exceed that of the original telephone and telegraph and, in fact, of electricity. There are more than one hundred million Internet connections right now and about a billion telephone connections. As the twenty-first century sets in on a world largely still resident in the nineteenth, the number of telephone connections is going to continue to increase, probably sharply. Ultimately most of those telephone connections, probably mostly cell phones, are going to include the internet. It is determining the way business functions, how nations operate, how the man on the street looks for a job, decides on a vacation, orders lunch or makes a date. It will change how we educate our children; treat our diseases; and how we relate to each other. It has already expanded the concept of personal circle from "here" to "wherever". A Wall Street stock broker can even now reach a cell phone client driving a camel in Turkey with the connection costing far less than the broker is going to spend for lunch. Networks are of ancient origin. The camel driver's ancestors also had a network. It was as fast as their camel, with the camel's range. The participants knew each other personally. The modern camel driver's network can be world wide, virtually instantaneous, and include people he never has and never will meet.

At a time when information is becoming a commodity, it is only useful if it is easily at hand which is specifically the certainty reinforced by the Internet. As digital equipment takes over all of the household utilities market, virtually all of the homes which have them will become connected to Web sites on the Internet for every day routines. With such a fantastic service inventory eventually offered to everyone, wisdom will become a matter of how it is used and opportunity an issue of how it's paid for.

Just as it is too early to predict the totality of the benefits and drawbacks of a dominating digital communications network, it is also too soon to judge the net balance of the two. Whether the e-net alienates people or involves them really has yet to be determined. Most other tools created by man had particular functions. A hammer could drive a nail or fire a rifle shell but it was basically a hammer. The Internet has no definable limiting purpose. In fact, its most distinctive character-istic is the flexibility but there is little doubt that its most rapidly expanding vista is interactions—people talking to each other across distance and setting. But even if the Internet has no virtue beyond sheer communication, it will transform the world of the next generation.

Summary:

Digital electronic networks are unique in human knowledge. Traditional net-works have formerly been dedicated associations of people with mutually agreed purpose. The Internet system has no horizon. Unlimited capacity, by itself, intro-duces a unique character. These constantly expanding e-net applications will, in the immediate future, change the priorities as well as the process of daily life. Lit-eracy will become a communal essential where once it was an individual achieve-ment. Indeed, the very word "literacy" has changed meaning. It once was defined as the ability to read and write on a stand alone basis. In tomorrow's world it will mean the ability to access the digital economy with reading only an implied con-dition.

Network scope is potentially so broad it becomes central to civilized infra-structure and as a result will become a point of great vulnerability to society. Even disregarding the national economic system, the networks will become so pivotal a part of civil function that network disablement might be more nationally cata-strophic than any other external attack. Electronic networks are a vital govern-ment asset which will very soon be protected from predation by international police forces. Efforts to regulate the networks are, in such a context, unavoidable and such early activities are already evident. But, regulation is almost a contradic-tion in terms because the central value of e-nets is the freedom which gives it such great commercial and individual value. Regulation complexity is further com-pounded by the nature of a system with no real physical location. Area restric-tions can easily be defeated by moving to another location, or even to another country. And finally, certainly not last, self regulation would require the viewer's cooperation—a very dicey alternative, to say the least, and certainly not one which anyone with criminal intent would observe.

The electronic network is in its infancy and so are the related problems. It has become an enormous source of personal entertainment and community, and at the same time an international mall and mail system. To be informed, they say, is to be empowered and information is specifically what the Internet provides with the most extensive availability in history. The social consequences of that new democracy will eventually reshape Shanghai Street. Main Street evolution is already restructuring.

Reading and Reference:

[1] *IEEE Spectrum* Jan.2001

[2] *And That's the Way It Will Be* C. Harper 0 8147 3576 2

[3] *The Business Internet and Intranets* Keen, Mougayar, & Torregrossa

[4] *Newsweek* January 1, 2000

[5] *Newsweek* 12/25/95 "This changes...everything" Levy & Hafner

[6] *The Internet travel Planner* Michael Shapiro 0 7627 0579 5

[7] AJC April 3, 2001

[8] *IEEE Spectrum* February, 1997 special issue: Electronic Money

[9] *Nation Magazine* June 21, 1999 P11

[10] Media Psychology Report 1999 McKenna & Bargh "Causes and Consequences of Social Interaction on the Internet"

[11] Journal of Housing & Community Development March/April 2001—
Bridging the Digital Divide

[12] *Science News* 5/4/2002 Bower

[13] NYTimes Thursday Aug.29, 2002

[14] *Civilizing the Internet* J.M.Kizza 0 7864 0539 2

[15] *Women@internet* Wendy Harcourt 1 85649 572 8

[16] *Digital Set-Top Boxes and Interactive TV* G.O'Driscoll 0 13 017360 6

[17] *Internet Public Library Handbook* Joseph Janes, David Carter 1 55570 344 5

[18] *Cast Your Net* E.f. Fagan 1 55832 189 6

[19] *Virtual Foreplay* E.E. Hogan, M.A. 0 89793 330 3

[20] *The Economist* November 23, 2002

[21] *Newsweek* January 1, 2000

[22] *Time Magazine* May 22, 2000

Conclusions

It is abundantly evident that this millennium ushered in a future painfully divergent from any historic experience. It isn't just how we will do things that will change. The revolution will include why we do them and with whom we do them and, indeed, whether we do them at all. Technology will have a direct bearing on social organization, jobs, health, religion, entertainment, politics, homes, associations,—all of that and more. And it isn't just the changes that will alter life, but the rate of change. It's going to be very uncomfortable for some, and, in the end, very advantageous for most.

When agriculture was invented, men could grow food outside their doorstep. It took ten thousand years for agriculture to spread throughout the world. When machinery was invented, it took only three hundred years for the new resource to dominate the world. The microprocessor did it in a single generation. Throughout that history, "wealth" referred only to physical assets. At this point in time much, if not most, of what is in the "new wealth" category is intellectual property. With all due respect to good intentions, it is abundantly clear that nations out of this mode are now, or are about to be marginalized. The good news is that the United States is the progenitor of the age and if the hegemony continues will accrue considerable advantage for Americans. Unless we make a horrendous mistake, this should be another American Century.

The intellectual paraphernalia supporting this advantage has spread so fast because it is truly a unique phenomenon in history. After a quarter of a century, new micro processing applications are being produced every day with most of them changing some aspect of life forever. New industries are being created every year, with the obverse side that old industries are being destroyed every day. The new jobs need more highly educated workers than most prior employment. The up side is that education, as well as the means of education, will themselves become new industries.

As a consequence of this revolution, the beneficiaries of the revolution will live both longer and healthier. We will very likely have more money than ever before which will permit more choices than any earlier time. Politics will be more individual and perhaps more personal.

Still, there are several underlying threats which are largely ignored. Until very recently, technologies encouraged redundancy—i.e., many sources for everything. For the very first time in history, there is now a technology with redundancy becoming outmoded. More and more of the world's vital systems are digitalizing and being hooked into common electronic networks. There will soon come a time where nothing, absolutely nothing, will be independent of that central nervous system. Power grids, traffic control, weather prediction, financial controls, military planning, politics, community functions, education, science, everything in fact described here, and many subjects omitted, will all become routed through this single pipeline. It's not a guess. It is a hard reality right now.

This condition is an incredible demonstration of the Law of Unintended Consequences. The Internet started as a federally funded defense network. From such a beginning, it has become a technology used by the military, by industries, by scientists, and by school children. Widespread computers and the Internet have, in fact, in two decades become crucial security assets to the entire industrial world and as such, susceptible to any system failure and therefore a prime target of attack by enemies. We ourselves are implicit participants to the inherent danger of a computer dominated millennial society because we tend to suspend human judgment in the face of contrary computer outputs. We are individually and collectively putting more and more of our vital assets into the decision making process of machines to which we attribute qualities of rationality and infallibility which we don't claim for ourselves.

Even aside from the dangers of system failure or criminal penetration, there must inevitably be a loss of privacy and independence which would be totally unacceptable to any previous generation of Americans. And there are other, perhaps more personal losses in this age. There is the real peril that while our children learn to read computer screens, they will forget the pleasures of reading a book. There is the risk of losing contact with a flesh and blood neighbor while having a lively contact with a remote stranger. There is the potential for substituting ever available digital entertainment for the enthusiasm of a live audience. There is the prospective of electronic shopping substituting for mall walking or any walking at all. In brief, there is a potential for unprecedented human disconnect in this extraordinary age of connection.

Still and all, the age is upon us and it is all we can do to manage our lives in the process. I suggest that the positives will outweigh the negative. The United States is a republic and our fate, as always, is in our own hands.

About the Author

Marty Blickstein has been a practicing engineer and business man for fifty years. He entered City College of New York (1942) as an engineering student, but the war became a first priority. He flew thirty five missions over Europe, acquiring three Air Medals and a Purple Heart along the way. After the war he entered Union College in Schenectady, once again majoring in Electronic Engineering. After graduating, he entered Brooklyn Polytech Institute, taking graduate courses, teaching, and working for Polytech Research and Development Corp. (PRD), a wholly owned school corporation.

He started his own business in 1959 and was active until 1980 when he sold his interest in the company. He "un-retired" as Chief Engineer/Product Managers position in a foreign (Japanese) company. He generated patents in the fields of electronics, microwaves, medicine, and even farming. He saw the world wide changes in the market place, in jobs, in training, and in outsourcing as they changed business, home, medicine, entertainment, communications, elections, and in fact, the world around us. He was spectator to the evolution of computers and the Internet from military purposes into household utilities. In short, he was a viewer to a social transformation which occurred during his own professional career as both a "participant" and a "bystander". During all of this time he traveled extensively in Europe, Asia, Japan, and America.

Mr. Blickstein now lives near Atlanta, Georgia where he still occasionally teaches this same material at Mercer University (Senior Extension), still travels, and still takes courses. He has one son who is a graduate Computer Scientist, living in New Hampshire and now working for Hewlett Packard.

Index

A

American
    medical 21
American Islamic communities 42
Arabic number 1
Armstrong 36
Assembly line
    medical 17
Association for Progressive Communications
    politics 81

B

Bank Cards 3
Billy Sunday 34, 35
BLS 113
brick and mortar bank 96, 138
Browser 158
Bureau of Labor Statistics 113
Buy American 6

C

Cable TV 165
capitation
    medical 25
career jobs 113
Chicago Mercantile Exchange 158
city planning 53, 57, 66, 68
Community of Strangers 170
Comprehensive Health Manpower Training
    Act of 1971 23
Computer Education 98
Copyright 157
Copyright Laws 157
Credit Cards 3

Croesus 1
currency market 158
cyber churches 38
cyber friendships 169

D

day care learning centers 98
Debit Cards 4
Digital 2
Digital Electronic Networks 177
Digital Medical Equipment 15
Direct Electronic Recording
    voting 87

E

e-commerce 119
Electric Cars
    community 65
Electronic Money 3
employment deficit 120
E-network 168
entry levels 118
extremist Web sites 173

F

failure of religion 45
Falwell 37
FCC 36, 37, 38, 162, 165
filter 164
Finney 34, 35
Fuel Cells 62

G

Gates, Bill 160

gender gaps 123
Genomics 13
global health 22
gold 1
GPS
    community 64
green vs. brown
    community 60
Gregor Mendel 13

H

hackers 173, 174
Health Insurance Portability and
    Accountability Act 18
HMO's 20
Home Lighting 54
Home Networking
    LAN 55
Home Offices 53
Home Schooling 100
house swapping 56
Hybrid Gas/Electric Car 65

I

IBA Community Development Corp. of
    Boston 173
Identity Cards 156
income stability 122
information revolution 9
intellectual assets 112
intellectual resources 8
Internet 157
    medical 15
Internet Community 74
Internet Interactivity 167
Internet Neighborhood
    Community 74
Internet Programming 166

is personal privacy
    medical 18
Islam 41

J

Jewish community 39
Judaism and Jewishness 39

K

K-12 104
key card
    voting 85

L

latchkey children 101
Law of Return 41
legal considerations 121
legal factors
    medical 17
lifetime jobs 121
Luddites 79
    voting 79

M

Malpractice Awards
    medical 19
Managed Care
    medical 20
market saturation 9
medical Rationing 24
men and women
    gender gaps 124
Money 1
money 3
Moody 34, 35

N

NATIONAL ID 87
National Patient Safety Foundation 29
neighborhood schools 102
Network crime 174

Network Security 162
new research 11

O

on-line election
    voting 86
Ottoman Empire 41
Out-sourcing 8

P

patent 3
Personal Behavior
    medical 30
Personal Medicine 14
Personal privacy 122
pharmacy 11, 12, 13, 14, 17, 21, 141, 146,
    163
photo voltaics 60
pilot Internet voting 91
Political Web 79
practice of learning 95
preachers 35
Price Control
    medical 20
privacy 5, 18, 56, 57, 86, 87, 122, 156, 162,
    168, 182
professional women
    politics 81
Provider Networks
    medical 26
Public Education 94
Public Housing 173
Public Transportation
    European Union 66

R

Radio and television 165
radio propaganda 80
Random Access Memory 159
Registering
    voting 86

replacement organs
    medical 14
Revivalism 34
Robertson 37

S

School 94
school texts 105
search engines 158
secondary energy sources
    community 72
Secularism 44
Security 7, 79, 87, 130, 132, 135, 137, 140,
    174
self-employment 108
Selling by Internet 166
Servers 158
Shopping malls
    community 57
short product market life 121
silver 1
Smart Cards 4, 156
Smart Equipment 23
smart equipment
    medical 23
Smart Phones 161
Society for Worldwide Interbank Financial
    Telecommunication 158
solar heating 61
Stalin 39
Standard Housing 56
Superconductors 63
supply side approach
    medical 23

T

telecommunity 58
terrorist 43, 159, 175
the Vanishing Voter
    elections 90

Time Shares 56
touch screens
    voting 87
trash
    community 69

U
uninsured population
    medical 21
unionized industries 123
unlimited demand and limited supply
    medical 24
upward mobility 6

V
Video Churches 38

video games 167
voting equipment
    digital 83
Vouchers 100

W
Wall Street 176
water as a limited resource
    community 68
working hours 121
workplace 113
World Monitor 162
World Wide Web 158

Y
Yiddish 39

0-595-31964-5

www.ingramcontent.com/pod-product-compliance
Lightning Source LLC
Chambersburg PA
CBHW021601280526
45784CB00001BA/448